SECOND EDITION

Dreaming Insights

A 5-Step Plan For Discovering the Meaning in Your Dream

Teresa Pollock.

SECOND EDITION

Dreaming Insights

A 5-Step Plan For Discovering the Meaning in Your Dream

Gillian Holloway, Ph.D.

Practical Psychology Press – Portland, Oregon

Dreaming Insights
A 5-Step Plan for Discovering the Meaning in Your Dream

Practical Psychology Press
P.O. Box 535
Portland, OR 97207
press@thrivenet.com
www.thrivenet.com/press/

Cover design: Amie Walter, Amiedesign
Book design and prepress: Kristin Pintarich, KP Services

10 9 8 7 6 5 4 3 2 1

Library of Congress Cataloging-in-Publication Data

Holloway, Gillian.
  Dreaming insights : a 5-step plan for discovering the meaning in your dream / Gillian Holloway.-- 2nd ed.
       p. ; cm.
Includes bibliographical references and index.
  ISBN 0-944227-27-9
 1. Dream interpretation. I. Title.
  BF1091 .H57 2001
  154.6'3--dc21

                                2001088457
                                Rev.

Acknowledgments

I wish to thank my friend Diane DiPrete for her excellent help in proofing the manuscript of this book, (any residual imperfections are the sole responsibility of the author), and for her constant encouragement and interest in the topic. I am grateful for the friendship and encouragement of Dr. Al Siebert, who has helped me to develop "computer courage" as well as writer's survival skills. Thanks to my brother Doug, for giving me a printer (effectively eliminating my final remaining excuse for procrastination). And special thanks to my mother, Pat, who has patiently listened to my enthusiastic explanations of life ever since she taught me how to talk.

Dedication

This book is dedicated to that aspect of self residing in each of us
that continually tries to shed light on the darkness,
connect the fragments of our understanding into a meaningful whole,
and reintroduce us to our abandoned talents and discarded loves:
to the dreamer within.

Contents

"I wonder what that dream meant..."

Sometimes the feeling that a dream has meaning will be so strong it will be an almost physical sensation, like having a forgotten name on the tip of your tongue. Whether or not you discuss such a dream, you are left with a haunting feeling of having been touched, of receiving communication from a deeper part of the mind. If the dream is particularly meaning-ful, it may float to the surface of your consciousness during the day, triggered by some word or event which seems oddly related to it.

The dreams which seem most puzzling are the most critical for us to understand.

Those dreams that stir us with the sensation of their impor-tance, yet challenge us to unravel their message are often the most valuable to understand. The subjective experience of *relevance* combined with the conscious inability to *recognize meaning* is always a powerful clue that a dream is significant. Any dream that feels important may indeed be vital—even more so *because* it is difficult to understand. Each of us has areas in life that we tend to deny or avoid understanding. Some of us have been taught that we cannot think and feel at the same time for example, so that any experience which would evoke both feelings and contemplation causes us to draw a blank. If a dream centers upon something that eludes the grasp of your conscious mind during waking life, you may find it tricky to examine the information in dream form as well. Yet the determination and courage required for the ex-ploration of dreams is well worth it.

Dreams, if understood, are a powerful resource for better understanding yourself and the complexities of your waking life. Dreams can offer insights about why you feel so strongly about certain things, what is really going on in your work setting, why relationships always seem so difficult, and what is meant by those stirrings of discontent that sometimes excite you and other times depress you. The part of your mind that creates your dreams has a stronger awareness of certain kinds of information, and certain levels of understanding than does your conscious mind. As a result, your dreams contain surprising insights and perspectives about your waking life, and the themes that are woven throughout your lifetime.

You may already have noticed some intriguing connections between your dreams and your experiences in waking life. Even people who have not made a study of dreams have the *intuitive* feeling that they hold meaning. Many who remember their dreams have had at least one experience of recognizing what was meant in a dream. It is a strange and exciting feeling to recognize the connections between dream images and experiences in waking life. This awareness can give you a feeling of greater depth in your life—a sense that events are interconnected in ways that are not always visible, but which nevertheless have impact and purpose.

You may have felt drawn to learn about dreams several times before, and only now have decided to make the time to do so. Or you may have a great deal of experience with dreamwork and find that your level of understanding has evolved and changed, so that now you crave more information or another perspective.

Methods for exploring dreams and interpreting their imagery are quite varied. Some developed out of the early approaches to psychotherapy, and those methods tend to be oriented toward uncovering pathology. As a result, even today many people approach the topic of dreamwork with the fear that some unfortunate character attribute will be uncovered by the process. In my work with the dreams of friends, students, and family, however, the reverse experience is by far more common.

Dreams tend to point out talents, gifts, and inner strengths which the conscious mind has either forgotten or ignored. You will not become involved in dreamwork and discover there is something "wrong" with you, but you may well be deeply moved by recovering aspects of yourself or talents you had long ago abandoned.

Other types of interpretation arose out of native folklore and religious teachings. These methods carry with them the necessity of familiarity with and belief in certain traditions and philosophies. Without a background in these schools of thought the methods of interpretation can be frustratingly complex and obscure. Many people have heard bits and pieces of information from differing approaches and have assumed that each "truth" came from the same source. Hearsay about these different processes can create confusion and even fear about understanding a particular dream's significance.

The approach I have developed and share with my students is geared toward personal growth and self-discovery. Using principles from contemporary psychology, as well as understandings about the language of the unconscious mind, you will be able to decipher and learn from the information that comes to you each night. This approach is really a *system* for recording and looking at dreams in a way that helps make their meaning more apparent.

If you have ever accompanied an outdoor guide on a journey, you know that such a person is able to see and recognize things in the woods that would be invisible to you and me. This is because they have cultivated the *skill* of looking at things in a way that permits them to see what is there. Similarly, uncovering meaning in dreams is largely a matter of practicing the skill of *looking at them in a way that allows you to see what is there.*

The method I will share with you in these pages is simple enough to give you an immediate experience of success, and profound enough to provide a framework from which you can dive off into deeper explorations as you feel ready. The steps are straightforward but effective, and the checkpoints insure that you examine your personal associations for the greatest possible accuracy. If you give yourself a little time to practice and explore dream interpretation, you will be pleased and surprised by how proficient you become, as well as by the depth of understanding revealed by your inner mind.

Whether you are a vivid dreamer with a excellent memory for rich details, or you are aware of the potential value of dreams but have yet to make much sense of them, I hope you will be able to enjoy and use these guidelines with ease. I believe there is a thread of destiny that runs throughout our lives, guiding us into places that hold potential gifts for us at specific times. Since this book has come into your hands, it is very likely that this is *your* time to explore and benefit from your dreams.

To improve dream recall, try the following steps:

♦ Decide to make the effort. Conscious determination filters down to the subconscious and helps to build a bridge between the states of awareness.

♦ Keep a pad of paper or tape recorder near the bed. Simple preparation is practical and also acts as a signal to your mind that you mean to follow through.

♦ Use the tag approach. Give the entire dream a name that stems from part of the action or a memorable moment. By writing down or recording the tag, you will be able to pull the entire dream out of your memory bank later when you want to record it.

♦ Write it down or tape record it. Don't try to decipher meaning as you record it. Simply get it down.

♦ Highlight the action, feelings, and any symbols that stand out to you. Put the dream aside and return to it later to interpret it.

♦ Avoid making the declaration that you don't remember. Memory is one of the most susceptible functions to autosuggestion; that is, we generally recall what we tell ourselves we remember, and "forget" what we direct ourselves to forget. If a dream eludes recall temporarily, rather than tell yourself "I can't remember," think, "I will remember it in a minute. It's coming back to me." This works surprisingly often, and is an excellent habit to improve memory skills in general. If you feel a little embarrassed making these announcements to yourself when they don't seem true, take consolation in the fact that no one else can hear you—only your subconscious mind will overhear and respond to what you declare to be true.

Chapter 2

Adjust Your Lens to See What is There

The assumptions you hold about dreams, and about *your* dreams in particular, will control the effectiveness of your efforts to uncover meaning. Assumptions about the nature of dreams, as well as about yourself, are actually the filter through which you look at the dreams you recall. Adjusting those assumptions is like focusing the lens on a microscope; what once appeared to be completely blank suddenly comes into view with clarity and definition, full of information and activity. At the present stage of understanding, certain generalities about dreams have become widely accepted and have proven most useful when working towards interpreting them. The three assumptions, or working constructs, are as follows:

1. Assume the dream has meaning, even if you don't see any when you first recall and record it.
2. Decide to accept and learn the language of dreams.
3. Empower yourself as the final authority about the meaning of your dreams.

Dreams come to us because they have something to say. Although they may appear to be comprised of a jumble of distorted images, or simply a playback of bits and pieces of recent experiences, *your dream is always an offering from the unconscious mind to the conscious mind.* It is in effect like an inter-office memo going from one department to another. The difficulty comes when we attempt to understand the dream using the language and rules of reasoning which apply to the "waking-reality department." For better or worse, dreams are created by a part of the mind which deals with things in a very creative, almost poetic manner. The key to understanding the insights and messages in dreams lies in learning to approach them on their own terms.

What does this mean? It means temporarily adjusting the way you *think* to allow the symbols, metaphors, and exaggerations in the dream to make sense. The language of dreams appears to be designed for greater expression than does our verbal language; and it is also a language capable of expressing things *for which there are no words.* Our verbal language is like a kind of cognitive short-hand which we use to condense and define things into manageable units of meaning. When we use our "normal" logic to try and understand our dreams, we often decide that our dreams seem "crazy," because we are looking at them through a viewfinder that blocks out most of their meaning. Remember that the language of dreams is all about revealing and unfolding meaning, while the language of conscious thought is about defining, and therefore *condensing* meaning.

To work most effectively with dreams, you will need to do something which, for some will feel like "becoming sloppy" in your thinking. A slight loosening of linear processes will help to get you used to associative thinking. You will become accustomed to searching for what dream elements *remind you of,* and sometimes the associations will be without satisfactory logic. This procedure can seem awkward and frustrating if you aren't accustomed to it. It takes courage to be willing to use a thinking process that seems foreign to you, but the rewards are well worth the effort. If you are *used* to associative thinking, this approach will seem like "old home week," and you will be thrilled to find a place where your "weird" way of looking at things really pays off! Either way, once you begin to get a handle on working with your dreams, you will find the process intensely pleasurable and fascinating. The information you uncover will be invaluable to you in self-understanding, the recognition of undercurrents at play in your life, and in acknowledging your talents and abilities.

Many people are astonished at the creativity and precision of their own minds when they begin to recognize the messages within their dreams. It is as if you discover an award-winning artist, poet, and playwright who lives within your psyche, and whose very purpose is to provide you with insights and personal resources to enrich your life.

You are the subject, the author, and the interpreter of your dreams.

One of the reasons working with dreams is so powerful is because *you are the best authority on your own life.* No friend, pastor, or therapist in the world has the depth of understanding about your experience that you do. Certainly it is important to let yourself reach out for guidance and counseling when you need it. But so often when we have difficulty finding the way out of a problem, or making a decision, it is because we aren't *consciously* aware of how much we know. Have you ever struggled with a decision you found particularly painful simply because you didn't have enough information to really know what to do? A great deal of subliminal information of which you aren't consciously aware is received and recognized by the unconscious mind, and it is offered to you at night in your dreams. Dreams are like a helping hand from your own mind shining a flashlight on the way out of the cave. They can reveal aspects of a situation that you had overlooked, or play out with the accuracy of a computer hypothetical scenarios of future results based upon current actions.

The more you focus upon your dreams, the richer and more profound they seem to become. The part of your mind which creates dreams is exceptionally sensitive and responsive. It is as if the part of your mind that acts as "dreammaker" learns how to work with you as you learn to work with it. Many people have reported to me that their dreams become more "user friendly" after they decide to learn more about them. This level of communication with your own psyche is a wonder to experience, and can lead to greater levels of confidence in other areas of life as well.

Think of dreamwork as a learning process as well as an adventure.

Working with dreams is valuable because the information they contain is useful in very real, practical ways, and because you will have great fun exploring them. It is not necessary to imbue the process with any particular philosophical significance or spiritual overtones, nor is it necessary to avoid those areas if they are already a part of your life. Understanding your dreams will strengthen your ability to create and to grow in whatever way you presently desire. You will have more success with the process if you are curious, respectful, and playful in your explorations.

Sometimes newcomers to dreamwork tend to be so serious about the possible implications within their dreams that they actually *block* some of their insights because of concern about uncovering deep psychological problems or weaknesses. It is not unusual for me to be approached by someone who is so troubled by the apparent content of a dream that she is driven to seek help uncovering its meaning. Disturbing dreams are important to examine, not merely because they may indicate trouble, but because the shocking quality of the dream was designed deliberately to get the dreamer to pay attention. As you will learn, frightening dreams are more often signs of important insights your mind wants you to consider than of impending danger.

Regardless of whether a dream was enjoyable or frightening (or whether you are embarrassed by the content of it), all dreams are valuable, and are ultimately offered to help. Don't ever let the quality of a dream "put you off" from working with it. Invariably further examination of the dream will diffuse the emotional intensity of it and will allow you to benefit from the meaning you discover.

Adopt a "learning orientation."

The process of understanding your dreams is just that; a process. It is important to adopt an orientation of learning skills for examining dreams in general, as well as hoping to decode any given dream in particular.

The benefits of this learning orientation are twofold. First it encourages experimentation without fear of "doing it wrong" because if you're learning you are entitled to make mistakes. Secondly, it allows for fluctuations in your results, because your goal is not to become an expert by Tuesday; it is to learn about your dreams. Whether you can "crack" the meaning of a dream or not your are still learning by recording and reflecting upon possible interpretations. Naturally, you want to be able to understand dreams when you choose to, but if you focus on the process of exploring them, you will take away any performance anxiety (especially if you are in a dream group), and attend instead to the likeliest techniques for bringing meaning to the surface. The more you practice, the more pleasurable you will find the process of exploration. Many dream enthusiasts feel that the exploration of a dream is a kind of deeply personal gift which they are able to give themselves, and share with others.

Assume all dreams have meaning.

It is easy to write off a certain dream as meaningless because it seems mundane, or because you can recall only a fragment. As understandable as this may be, it is a mistake you want to avoid. Even more commonly, students will *excuse* the dream from containing any meaning because they recognize portions of it as originating from day material; such as a television show they watched or a conversation they overheard that day.

One of the most fundamental things to understand about dreams is that *even though your mind "borrows" material from your day to use as props in your dream, this doesn't mean that the prop caused the dream.*

As children, most of us were told by parents that our bad dreams were caused because we watched scary movies. This is partly true in that emotions stirred up by movies, television, or art of any kind do tend to become part of our dreams. And often the dream will use whole chunks of material that appear to come straight out of the movie. However, *the movie is not the meaning of the dream.* I stress this, because even the serious student will occasionally stun me by interpreting a dream featuring "blue wallpaper" as having been caused by some blue wallpaper they saw recently. This is an easy mistake to make unless you keep in mind what most dream experts agree upon: *all dreams have meaning.* There are dreams that appear to have been compiled from what we call "day residue," and to some extent one of the jobs of dreams is to sort out excess stimuli and excess emotion that is stirred up during the day. However, the characters, symbols, and actions of the dream are not thrown in arbitrarily: they are selected because they mean something. If you are not moved to work with a certain dream then admit to yourself that you are not interested in it right now, but do not put it aside because you recognize in it the story line from an episode of *LA Law*. You have seen a lot of television and entertainment in your lifetime, and your dreammaker is free to select from any source for material. The reasons for this particular selection are due to the meaning the dream is trying to convey. If you disregard the artistry of the selection of any part of your dream as having come about through convenience, then you will cut yourself off from the actual meaning of the selection.

Following up on this perspective is another critical point to remember. Just as the dream and its contents and characters have meaning and are not "accidents," so the placement of the dream during your night's array of dreams has meaning too. You may be thinking "Oh no, this is getting too complicated. Not only do I have to remember the dream, but I have to remember where it fell among several dreams!" If you can, yes. Why is this important? Because the mechanism of dreams is so sophisticated that if you don't see the meaning in one dream, you will be given a clue by the juxtaposition of one dream to another. This is yet another example of your first rule of thumb in dreamwork: assume that everything is intentional and meaningful. Work with what attracts you most, but assume that everything about your dreams is potentially meaningful.

Here's an example of a young woman who was unable to recognize the meaning of an individual dream, although its message was later revealed by the relationship of one dream to another:

Lynn was an ambitious and savvy modern woman who had been in a tumultuous relationship for over a year with a man she adored, but who had trouble handling her independence. She came to me because of her concern with a recurring nightmare.

> *I am alone in the house and feeling fine when I realize that there is a monster outside in my back yard. I rush around and bolt all the doors and windows. I feel very nervous and scared. There is something familiar about the monster, but I don't know*

what it is. I can't understand how the monster got in my yard without my knowing it. I think I have things secured when it starts crashing into the windows to break in and get at me. I can only hope that it won't be able to break though the windows or door. Then I go into another dream.

If Lynn had not mentioned the transition: "Then I go into another dream," we might not have been alerted that her next dream might have bearing on the nightmare. Here is the second dream:

I am about to go somewhere with Jay. We are very close and happy. I think how lucky we are to have found each other, and that the bad times are not important. I tell him about the monster that has me worried, and he holds me close to him.

Either dream, on its own, might have been interpreted according to its content. Together, they worried me a great deal. I asked Lynn for her other recollections of the nightmare, and sure enough, after each episode of the monster, she immediately went into a dream of being with Jay, and telling herself not to worry about the bad times with him. Her description of her relationship with Jay was that he had almost a split personality: a vengeful, jealous, enraged side, and the loving, charming, humorous side with which she was in love.

I believed that her dreams were giving Lynn a dramatic warning that the "monstrous" side of Jay was, in fact, a real danger to her, but she was not able at that time to accept the interpretation. Lynn denied that her boyfriend could ever do anything to hurt her, and she decided to remain in the roller coaster relationship. (Most of us have difficulty accepting an unwanted truth, and no one should be blamed because they are simply not ready to accept what their dreams are fairly shouting at them.) It was not until Jay became violent during one of his fits of rage, striking Lynn and destroying many of her belongings, that she was able to recognize the monster in her dreams and decide to leave the relationship.

Your dreams reflect the way your inner self experiences life events.

You may wonder why dreams don't just "come out with it," and give a more literal example of their meaning. One reason is that you are living the literal meaning in your waking hours, and you may be refusing to see the truth, as Lynn was. In such cases, *the action of the dream will be tailored to your hesitancy to see the truth.* Someone will be disguised, or you will be blindfolded, or other elaborate means will be used to communicate in a concealed way what it going on. Dreams are usually a reflection of how your inner self experiences what is going on. Lynn's dreams reflected her inner experience pretty aptly: there was the man she loved, and then there was the monster that frightened her. *She experienced them as separate entities,* and her dreams depicted them as such. They also depicted Lynn telling herself not to worry about Jay. The subconscious mind sees things in an artistic, metaphorical way. It speaks a language of symbols, metaphors, and exaggerations. By accepting and working with this style of communication, rather than considering it merely a lurid distortion of "reality," you will speed up your ability to recognize important information as it is presented to you.

Your dreams are almost always about your current life, or something affecting your current life.

The final critical point to keep in mind as you examine your dreams is that *they are nearly always about something that is going on currently in your life.* Even if you dream about something that happened when you were five years old? Yes, you are dreaming about that incident because something is occurring in your life that is emotionally or symbolically similar to what was going on in your life then.

It may be that the dynamic created during a childhood incident is troubling you in your current relationship, or that your new job is violating you in some way that reminds your subconscious of the way you were violated as a child.

Even if a dream seems to be about a "past life," the reason you are having the dream is because aspects of the past are paralleling something in your current life, or there is something you need to look at which is being "played back" for your edification. This is a rule you can count on. Even precognitive dreams come at certain times which have significance. They may be about future events, but they usually come when they can make the most impact and be most useful to you, or when you are most open to their message because of your present circumstances.

The more willing you are to explore the truth, the more fruitful your explorations will become.

Some traditions teach that if you travel toward wisdom by learning new skills and keeping an open mind, then the wisdom you seek will meet you halfway by moving toward you through events and people you encounter. This seems to hold true in dream analysis. As you become more adept and open-minded in your interpretations, your dreams will become more informative and accessible. Think of the difference between talking with someone who is ignoring you, and talking with someone who stops and gives you their full attention, even asking questions in order to better understand. Don't you tend to go into more detail, and reveal much more to the second type of person? It is natural for the part of your mind responsible for creating dreams to respond to your interest. Keep in mind that this is a process of one part of the mind learning from another. Both aspects of your mind possess certain kinds of consciousness, and certain kinds of intelligence.

Thus there is even a level of interactive learning which takes place, in which you will become aware that you are dreaming, and will discuss prior dreams with characters in your present dream. This is a little bit like a performer addressing the "4th wall" in a production, saying to the audience: "I just hate to play in costume dramas." The richness of your dreams will begin to give you an idea of the level of sophistication and complexity of which your mind is capable. As one student told me: "I can't believe my mind is so *deep!*"

When you look at your waking life, you see it through the filter of your hopes, fears, expectations, and beliefs. Your inner mind however, sees your waking life in a different way because it is not restricted by the viewfinder of your conscious beliefs. Thus you may notice things in the reflection of your life (the dream), which were invisible to you in your experience.

This is one reason why sharing dreams with others is a tremendous help in uncovering their meaning. Because you are often dealing with unconscious material, it is almost natural to be more confused by your own dreams than another person would be. For this reason, it is an excellent idea to give yourself a chance to work with a dream group or a dream analyst at least briefly. Other people notice the oddities in your dreams, while you may be distracted by certain portions of the dream and fail to notice something you just took for granted.

For example, you dream that you come home and there is a huge desk in the living room of your house. It is the size of a car, and takes up all the space in the living room. You might assume (correctly) that something is out of proportion in your life. If, however, another dream student found out from you that the dream desk is like the desk you use at work, we would wonder if you are letting your work-life cramp and crowd out your "living" space and time. You may have known that the desk was like your work desk, but it may not have struck you as meaningful. Others could point out that this selection was made in place of hundreds of other objects your dreammaker could have chosen, and thus it is significant. Working on your dreams with others can allow you to uncover specific meanings encoded in props and settings, while solitary exploration is often limited by your own recognition of relevance.

Adopting a theory is less effective than learning a skill.

There are so many aspects of meaning in dreams that it is easy to be overwhelmed by trying to understand them all. Matters are made still more confusing by the traditions of certain psychologists and researchers who claim there is just one way (their own) to analyze dreams. If you are deeply curious about dreams, I recommend that you read the thinkers on the subject who attract you, and consider their opinions and insights as a smorgasbord. Take what you want and leave the rest.

The more opinions you hear, the more you will recognize generalizations they all contain, and it is the generalizations which may be relied upon regardless of the theoretical school from which they stem. Recognizing the general tendencies of dreams and understanding their probable nature will give you a head start on unraveling their meaning for yourself.

Be cautious about adopting a rigid adherence to one school of thought—this may cause you to narrow your own ability to recognize important clues to meaning. As with any science or type of inquiry: what you expect and believe to be true will affect what you are able to uncover. Under the circumstances, I believe it is wiser to err on the side of open-mindedness, rather than risk blotting out your own genius. As you become more experienced in working with dreams, you will learn to recognize the pleasant "click" of understanding which accompanies an accurate interpretation. If you enjoy puzzles or mystery stories, you will recognize a similar thrill of comprehension to the one you get when you accurately solve a "whodunit." If you are told an interpretation by someone else, regardless of how expert they are reputed to be, and the analysis doesn't seem to fit your subjective experience, it is very likely that the interpretation is either inaccurate, or incomplete.

Generalizations about dreams are helpful short-cuts, not iron-clad rules.

Have you ever heard someone say that all the characters in a dream are really just parts of yourself? This approach is frequently talked about and can be a useful avenue to explore when examining a dream. However, it can cause dreamers to miss important insights by convincing them to stop short of the real meaning. *Sometimes* the characters in dreams do represent parts of the dreamer, but to force that interpretation is to misunderstand a great many of your dreams. The rule of thumb for recognizing characters is this: describe what the person or creature is like, and then ask yourself who that description reminds you of. Once you get the description *off the surface of the dream character, and look at the descriptors separately,* you will be able to recognize who the character represents in your life. If the description fits your next door neighbor, then that is likely who the character represents. If the description best fits an aspect of yourself, you may interpret the character as representing that aspect of your own personality.

Chapter 3

Your Dream Journal: A Tool For Remembering

Keeping a journal is the best way to train yourself to recall your dreams and to get into the habit of examining them. The manner in which you go about this is up to you. If you are a meticulous person, you will want to have a highly organized, structured dream journal. I suggest you use a large lined notebook, because in addition to writing down the dream, you will be making a lot of notes about your associations to images and actions.

If you are a hit-and-miss person (I like to think of it as *spontaneous),* get yourself any kind of notebook that is comfortable and convenient, and attach a pen to it so that when you are ready to write you won't be distracted by having to search for a writing instrument. Especially when you are sleepy and your dreams are *right there*, you don't want to have anything delay your recording them.

There are many attractive "dream journals" on the market now, and many are fun and magical-looking. It isn't necessary to have something stylish to write in, although the more fun you make this, the more likely you will be to make it a habit. Whatever you use, make sure that it has enough room to write all you wish, and to record associations and thoughts about the dreams as well. One difficulty with some journals is that they are bound like a book or a diary, and won't stay open on their own. There will be many times when you will want to reflect on the dream in its entirety, and being able to see it all on one page will be a great help to you. Most students find that a spiral notebook is useful, wears well, and provides ample writing space. The rule of thumb here is to do what suits you. If you want to decorate your journal and turn it into an art project, by all means do so. If making a big deal of it intimidates you, then keep your relationship to your journal a light and friendly one. I use a spiral dream journal with a smooth-writing pen clipped onto the outside, and keep it under my bed. I have tried recording dreams into my computer (for the sake of neatness), but the time-lag between awakening and turning on the computer has proven to be a hindrance. It is important to jot down your dreams while they are fresh. Don't try to analyze them while you are recording them. Your first job is simply to make sure they don't evaporate as your day takes over. Record them as best you can. If you remember only an image or a scene, write that down. Never discount something because it seems like merely a fragment.

Make it easy for yourself— so you will do it!

Some people like to talk their dreams into a tape recorder, and transcribe them later. If that appeals to you, give it a try. *Gauge the appropriateness of your approach by whether you tend to avoid it or not.* If you get too technical, or make things too much like work, the tendency is to get away from keeping the journal. Also, if you have perfectionistic tendencies and set standards for yourself that are tiring to live up to, you may give up the whole project. Keeping a dream journal should be fun and intriguing.

You needn't record a dream every morning if you don't want to, although the more you are able to "catch" during the beginning the stronger will be the connection you build with that part of yourself. Some nights you will recall several dreams. You may think of such times as hitting the jackpot. When you have the opportunity to look at a number of dreams from one night, I recommend that you take advantage of it. Often you will be offered several different points of view about a certain situation or relationship by receiving several very different dreams in one night.

The more you record dreams, the more succinct and accurate your descriptions will become, and the less effort will be involved in the process. Allow yourself to write in a natural style, without editing or worrying about grammar. Abstain from thinking critically about the process. People who enjoy writing tend to enjoy the process and to write more elaborate descriptions. People who feel self-conscious about writing, or about the significance of their dream images, may tend to discount certain aspects of the dream because the meaning is not readily apparent. While you needn't become fanatical about writing down every minute detail of the dream, you are doing yourself a disservice if you deliberately leave out colors or images simply because they don't, at the time, strike you as meaningful. The important thing is to preserve your dream as you experienced it, so that later you can derive benefit from your understanding of it.

Journal Entries

Following is a sample page of what you might want your journal to look like:

Date _____

Day Events: I was told today that they are bringing in a new supervisor at work. I am worried that this will effectively put me even farther back in line for promotion.

Dream Question: Show me more about my feelings about my work situation. Are they valid?

Dream: I am trying to open the front door of the office building, but find that it is locked. I look for my key and cannot find it. I turn to find my car to race home for a key, and I can't find where I parked my car. I finally get into an older model car that is kind of a junker. I awaken feeling distraught.

Analysis: The dream shows me dealing with a work situation, so I can assume that my issue is being addressed by the "dreammaker." I am facing a locked door, feeling distraught, and blocked by my lack of a key. When I go to drive home, my car is an early model, junkie old thing. This indicates that I feel my ego-self has slipped down several notches. I am indeed feeling threatened that my access at work is being blocked, and that I will be stuck in an out-of-date arrangement. This change may mean that I will be right back where I was when I drove that type of car.

Each time you record a dream in your journal, you will want to date the entry. Some researchers recommend that before going to bed at night you jot down a couple of thoughts about the events of the day. These can be entered under the heading "day notes," or "day events," or "today...." These notes can give you a head start on understanding the dreams which occur during that night. And they can serve as a memory signal to your own mind that shows you intend to remember and record your dreams the following morning. Realistically, however, the practice of writing in the journal evening and morning is asking for quite a commitment. It may work for you to make some notes about your current life situation after you record a dream, or alternatively, to mention what your predominant thoughts were as you went to sleep.

For example, a young woman named Sarah told me that after dreaming repeatedly one night about a disheartening work situation, she remembered that her predominant thoughts as she fell asleep were about her relationship with her boyfriend, and the pain she felt about his lack of emotion towards her. Upon examination, we saw that the patterns at work which caused her pain—a tendency to devalue herself in an attempt to win approval—were present as well in her relationship with her lover. She recognized she was making herself smaller and smaller in their relationship in an mis-guided attempt to give her partner the confidence to express his feelings. Her dreams showed Sarah becoming mentally side-tracked and emotionally exhausted by her patterns of interaction. Had she not remembered her thoughts prior to falling asleep, it would have been very easy to connect these dream images only to her work life, and to overlook the important link to her personal life.

Using present tense will bring your dream memories back to life.

As you write down your dreams, and later if you tell them to others, I recommend you recount them using the present tense. Rather than saying *I went to the door and opened it, and there was my first grade teacher.* Say: *I go to the door, and open it, and there is my first grade teacher.*

Writing in the present tense may seem awkward at first, but it is a marvelous tool for getting yourself to remember the dream more accurately. Also, it tends to associate the dreamer back into the *experience* of the dream. How the dream *felt* to you as you experienced it is one of the most important clues to its meaning. The subjective feeling seems to be the part that fades the fastest, and beginners tend to leave out their feelings when recounting their dreams to others. Yet it is your feelings which can often most accurately tell you what your dream is about. Here is an example of a dream "fragment" from a man named Paul.

> *I am standing in a field. The sun is beating down on me. I am surrounded by flowers on all sides.*

Looking at this superficially it seems like a pleasant dream fragment. When Paul *leaves out* his feelings during the experience, anyone helping him decipher the dream would expect it to have pleasant associations. However, when I asked Paul to associate into his feelings in the dream, he had this to say:

> *I feel caught in the field. The flowers look beautiful, but I am uneasy about them surrounding me like that. The sun is beating down on me and I am anxious because there is no cover or shade. I am embarrassed about being afraid of a bunch of flowers, yet I sense that they are not what they appear to be.*

What a difference feelings make in the meaning of a dream! Knowing what Paul's feelings were about this nature scene, we were able to connect them to his vague sense of unease about his new job situation. There, "everything looked rosy," but Paul had the feeling that "everything was not as it seemed to be." He was being offered more perks than he expected, and he was also encouraged to sell the public on something that looked good, but about which he wanted further information. Whenever he tried to get the facts about the reality of the situation, he received "heat" from the other employees. This was always done in such a smiling, radiantly phony way that Paul tended to doubt his own misgivings. The dream fragment was reflecting back to Paul the awkwardness of the situation, as well as showing him through his feelings that his concerns were worthy of consideration.

Make it a point to record the feelings you have in the dream.

If you are working with a dream group, dream analyst, therapist, or if you are studying your own dreams, be sure to include your feelings during the dream, as well as your reactions to it afterward, in your record or journal. These recollections (as we will examine in the chapter on interpretations) can often serve as a short-cut to identifying the meaning of the dream. Being thorough about recording feelings will also take much of the fear out of working with dreams, as you will begin to see the way in which dream language uses feelings to underline and emphasize meaning.

Emotions in dreams act in much the same way as dramatic music does during movie scenes. Both pull us into the action, and we know something is up in a movie (even before the hero) by the intensity of the suspenseful music. Emotions in dreams act as a kind of visceral neon sign saying: "THIS PART IS IMPORTANT!"

Try to achieve a balance between recording as much as possible at first, and staying comfortable and playful about your dreamwork. When you are pressed for time, or you simply don't feel like working with your dreams, don't force yourself, or feel guilty about your choice. The purpose of dreamwork is to add insight, enjoyment, and ease to your present life. If the process involved is making you feel just the opposite, then that is a signal to reorient to the overall goals of life-improvement, and loosen up on your day-to-day demands on yourself.

Leave room in your journal for comments about the dreams.

After you write down a dream, leave some blank space around it in which to jot down comments about your interpretation. In chapter four you will learn which points to highlight or underline and how to use them to uncover the dream's meaning. If you make a practice of recording, underlining, and reflecting on your dreams you cannot fail to begin making accurate associations about them. The accumulation of several dreams and your understanding about them is invaluable to building skill in dreamwork.

After a while you will notice repetitions of certain images and themes. For example one woman noticed that a stove often appeared in her dreams and that sooner or later in the action she would move something from the rear of the stove to the front. This image meant little to her, since she didn't like to cook, and seldom used a stove in her waking life. The recurrence of the symbol and the action over time though led her to believe that the image was an important one. By looking at the action she took and the recurring symbol of the stove more closely, she was able to recognize why her dreammaker was using the symbol so frequently. In each of these dreams she was taking something off the back burner and putting it up front. This woman had been waiting years to start the career she had always longed for, and seldom allowed herself even to think about it, or to practice the skills involved. (This was one reason why the stove was utilized as a symbol, since it represented something she "simply didn't do" in life—cooking.) The dreams were telling her over and over that the time was now right for her to take her ambition off the back burner and bring it right up front. In her case, the number of times this symbol appeared in her dreams was the tip off to its relevance, and she would not have noticed the recurrence if she had not been keeping a dream journal.

Accept the dreams as you record them.

The attitude you take towards something affects your ability to work with it. If you find yourself thinking "this was a dumb dream, and it doesn't have anything to do with me" as you go to record it, those thoughts will affect your ability to recall it accurately, and will tend to block off your deepest associations to the content and imagery. Practice the discipline of acceptance (a challenge, in any arena), by refraining from labeling the relevance of a dream before you understand what it was about. Some people call this "being non-judgmental" or "uncritical." However you think of it, summon up the resolve to treat your dreams as if they are important, helpful and purposeful—and you will find they "open" to your inquiries much more easily.

Points to remember about recording your dreams:

◆ **Make your journal convenient and easy to use**.

◆ **Approach the study of your dreams with discipline, but also with playfulness.** Launching into this with grim determination tends to close off your ability for creative thinking. You will need your creativity to understand the astonishing artistry of your dreams.

◆ **Know that whatever you uncover will be advantageous to you.** *Your dreams are on your side.* Sometimes dreamers come to me in great embarrassment about the content of their dreams. Don't be afraid of your dreams. They are always a gift that is meant to help you.

◆ **It is better to be consistent about your dreamwork than to be compulsive.** As it is with anything else, going overboard for a short time will be of little use to you. Working on your dreams regularly, but perhaps with less intensity, will open up rich avenues of understanding and empowerment to you. Enjoy the process, and don't criticize yourself for what you *don't* do!

Chapter 4

Dream Language

Because the language used by the "dreammaker" is different from the language we commonly use to think and reason, there is a challenge inherent to the discovery of meaning in dreams. However, there are patterns that appear to be quite consistent within dreams, and we can use these consistencies to learn the language of dreams, and thus to decipher their meaning.

The simplest way of recognizing the meaning of dreams is to examine the following elements within them: **action-metaphors, exaggerated emotions, and symbols.**

Action metaphors are wonderful clues to meaning. The metaphor is reflected by what you are doing during the dream, or the main action taking place.

If you are being stalked by an ominous force, then the action metaphor is *having something come after you in a threatening way.* In what way in your current life are you being stalked? If you are wandering lost across a barren landscape in your dream, you may have recently moved into a city where you know no one, or you may have divorced and altered your life-style so that it is unrecognizable. The action metaphor of *wandering and being lost* is your clue. When you have isolated that part of the dream, then take the action out of the dream context and look at it. If you are fighting for your life against unknown assailants, take that action element aside and look at it. *You're fighting for your life.* That much is safe to assume. This relates to something that threatens your life as you now know it, or where the danger to you is greater than you had imagined, or where a part of your identity is being threatened. Where in your waking life is your survival on the line? Similarly, if you dream of starving to death or wasting away, lift that out of the dream story and look at it on its own. *You're not getting nourishment, and you're beginning to lose your life.* That doesn't mean necessarily that you are in physical danger of dying, but that some vital part of yourself is dying off as a result of this lack of nourishment. Here is an example of the way an action metaphor can lead you to recognize meaning.

Immediately after graduate school I worked at a job I loathed. It was extremely stressful and contributed to many minor health problems as a result of my becoming run-down and generally unhappy. During the year I worked there I dreamed several times of being murdered. The action metaphor was that *I was being destroyed by something.* One dream in particular was especially troubling:

> *I am in a building with several of the people from my office. I am being murdered by someone who takes out the brains of women when he slaughters them. As I struggle against him, my foot slips on something. I look down, and there is a woman's brain on the floor—the remains of one of his more recent victims.*

The **action metaphor** here was that of losing my life to a malevolent force. Specifically, I was being murdered in a way that involved butchering my brain. (Since the characters were co-workers, I had a hint that the dream was about my work setting.) However, by simply stating the action metaphor, I could have identified the source of the dream. Where in life was I feeling "murdered," and as if my brain were being taken out? It was clear to me that this was one more in a series of dreams depicting me being destroyed by my work setting. The owner of the company was so destructive with his employees that we coined a nickname for him that was derivative of the famous sadist, the Marquis de Sade. The dream's use of women as victims had specifically to do with the company's treatment of women (and their brains).

To get a handle on action metaphors, just take a look at what you are doing in the dream. Are you fighting? Loving? Struggling? Crossing a bridge? Going through a barrier? Warning someone? Vomiting? Whatever you are doing, you can take a fairly direct metaphor from your dream action and use it to discover the association to your waking life.

When you are working at uncovering the metaphor within your dream action, ask yourself the following question:

"What am I really doing/experiencing here?" Get a one-or-two word description of action verbs to use in your interpretation. then consider the feelings in the dream.

Exaggerated emotions

One of the things that frightens people most about their dreams is the intensity of the feelings involved. Someone who may experience something mildly embarrassing during the day may dream that night of being forced to take part in a stage sex show. The dreamer will be so shocked and horrified by the dream that they may not make the association to the rather minor embarrassing incident the day before. Dreams with lurid sexual scenes, or dreams of extreme violence tend to frighten people, and make them wonder if they are suddenly experiencing some neurotic problem.

It will help you to keep in mind that dreams usually exaggerate the emotions you feel (and refuse to feel) during the day. One of the functions of dreams may be to keep us emotionally aware. It is natural, even practical sometimes, to put off emotional reactions to events, particularly when those reactions are unpleasant. Dreams, however, "catch" the feeling, even when the conscious mind is able to avoid recognition of it during waking hours, and the feeling will appear in your dreams, often amplified several emotional decibels. This amplification takes place in order to attract your attention, and as a response to hidden or suppressed emotion.

Dreams often allow you to play out emotions that simply wouldn't be appropriate to express (or even to entertain) in waking life. You may find yourself doing and feeling things that you would never think of doing in your waking life. This does not mean that your moral philosophy or political convictions have slipped, or are less than deeply held. Rather your dreams are allowing your impulses and even forbidden thoughts to follow some kind of evolution in order to release them from your system. Children often dream of monsters who may actually be depicting the "monstrous" side of their parents. In most households, criticism of parents is simply out of the question. For a child, the feeling that "today Mommie is just out to get me for some reason" will have to be suppressed. But that night the child will dream about just such an experience, probably with Mommie disguised, so as to allow the child to feel his feelings. In this way dreams act as a balancing system for the psyche, validating experiences that might otherwise have been denied due to cultural or other external pressures.

Dreams can also act as warning signals for our health and well-being. They reflect back to us situations, patterns and trouble spots that we apparently are unable to recognize in our waking hours. The more dangerous the situation to our well-being (physical, emotional, social or spiritual) the more dramatic and memorable will be the dream. In addition, the dreammaker seems to amplify the signal when previous dreams were not understood or attended to. This is a curious and often amusing quality to dreams. However, it doesn't feel amusing when you are having ghoulish and frightening night-mares.

Repressed emotion is often painful, and intense. When you examine it however, it subsides.

If you are dreaming of running away from something scary and horrible, the feeling may have been of *danger, and trying to escape.* The dream situation may well be more intense than your waking situation, but there is always a parallel. If you dream of reaching out to your spouse and he or she walks by without acknowledging you, then *your feeling is of being ig-nored by someone who is supposed to love you.* What does that remind you of in your waking life?

Sometimes the feeling you have when you *examine* a dream is different from what you experienced *during* the dream. *The feeling to use for interpretation is the emotion you felt during the dream.* Many times the content of a dream will shock you, or you will find it disquieting because it is about a taboo subject, or because you are alarmed by possible interpreta-tions. Don't worry about censoring your dreams. They can't be censored. Most of us have heard about theories of wish fulfill-ment; that dreams provide us with the things we desire in our waking life. Sometimes that is the case, but it is much more frequent that dreams *reflect* what we already have in our waking hours.

For example, if you dream of sexual incest it doesn't mean you secretly desire that type of intercourse. It is much more likely that you are experiencing peculiar enmeshment at work, or that you are dating someone who is so like a relative of yours that you feel almost guilty about being with him or her. Or possibly you are involved in doing something you feel is wrong, but you find it easier to "go along with it" than to say no. The emotional language of dreams is very basic, very intense, and startling. Your dreams will tell you very vividly when you are feeling violated, exposed, starved, or uplifted.

Symbols, the third element, are tricky to work with, precisely because so many definitions of their meaning exist. For instance, if you are dreaming of swimming in a pool, some experts would say that you are dreaming about emotion; others would say that water is always representative of knowledge; still others would say that water represents the unknown. Any of these interpretations would provide you with quite different understandings. So how are you to assign a meaning to something that appears in your dream?

A good place to begin is to reflect on what the object is to *you.* This is really the most accurate way to interpret the appearance of an object or setting. It is easy to take your understanding of something for granted, without realizing your association is really particular and personal. Since I cannot swim, I consider the water to be an element that is foreign and possibly dangerous. However, when I am learning a new area of study, and I dream of taking swimming lessons and doing very well, it is likely that the dream is reflecting my pleasure and confidence in that new learning. During a particularly rocky period in a romantic relationship, I dreamed of sailing with my boyfriend over shark-infested waters. This dream, I believed, was reminding me that there were hazards to our happiness under the surface of things, and in fact, this proved to be true.

It *is* entirely possible that in different dreams, the same object will have different meanings. It is necessary to check in with your own description of the object, consider the popular interpretations, and then test the associations to determine what fits for you. This kind of approach can be maddening if you are used to a more linear type of problem-solving. However, the more you do this, the easier and more exciting it will become for you. What appears from the outside to be "intuition," is actually just a different way of thinking. This is something that develops quite rapidly when exercised, and will prove valuable in many other areas of life as well.

To determine the symbolic meaning of an object in a dream, ask yourself the following questions:

- What function does it serve? What quality or property does it possess?
- Who or what kind of person would use it?
- Do you have something similar in an area of your waking life?
- Was there a time in your life when you would have used or been around this type of object? Are there similarities between that time and your *current* situation?

While symbols can be exciting and impressive purveyors of meaning, I recommend that you work with them to the best of your ability. If the meaning remains unclear, simply set them aside for a while. Frequently the real mystery of a dream is solved by getting a sense of the action-metaphor, and in bringing your feelings to the surface. Symbols often then fall into place.

Don't try to jump to conclusions before you have examined the meaningful parts of your dream.

One of the ways that we frustrate ourselves when attempting to analyze dreams is by prematurely attempting to link the dream to waking reality. It is seldom realistic to take the actions and content of a dream as they appear and try to apply them to waking reality. It simply won't make sense. People in dreams don't act the way they would in waking life, the same laws of reality don't apply to both situations, so you are going to run into confusing areas if you try to go directly from dream to reality.

Remember, your dream is speaking to you in metaphorical language, using action metaphors, exaggerated emotions, and symbols to depict conditions in your current life. When you take time to look at these elements, you begin to recognize the aspects of your life which they represent. Lets examine the dream of a charming woman I know named Candy (not her real name) who had been troubled with the following recurring nightmare for some time.

> I am flying on a big jet. Instead of sitting with the other passengers, I am up in the control cabin with the captain. It looks like the plane is going to go down. I am terrified. I am going to be destroyed. We do go down and crash. Many of the passengers are killed. But I am fine. I am perfectly all right, and I get out of the plane and walk away.

The jet was one of the main **symbols** in this dream, and I asked Candy what a jet was to *her*. Candy's description of a jet was that it was a *popular form of business transportation,* something everyone seemed comfortable with, but which she found a little unnatural.

One of the other obvious **symbols** of the dream is that Candy is seated *at the controls* of the plane, not back with the other passengers as would be more typical. Whenever the dream setting and action *differs from what you would expect in waking life*, you are being given an excellent hint. Cherish the apparently illogical aspects and sudden inconsistencies of your dream; these are always good clues to meaning.

The **exaggerated feeling** in the dream is that *Candy is facing her own destruction.* As always, the feeling is one of the best links to the actual waking situation the dream is depicting. After getting the descriptions of the other aspects of the dream, you can use the feeling to make the link back to your waking life. Don't be tempted to make that link before you have gathered a full description though, or you will simply target the life situation the dream is about, but miss the message the dream has to offer you.

The **action metaphor** is that Candy is *heading for a crash* and she assumes it will mean her destruction. However, a critical element of the action metaphor is that *Candy survives the plane crash. She is perfectly fine.*

Candy had asked me for help because this was a recurring dream and it frightened her. She correctly guessed that its message for her was important. Her main concern was that it was a warning of impending death due to a plane crash. Though pre-cognitive dreams do occur, I had no fear for

Candy in that regard because at the end of the dream she always walked away from the wreckage without a scratch. (In this case Candy found the exaggerated emotion of her fear so riveting that she did not take note of her safety at the end of the dream. This is why it helps to have others involved in your dreamwork. Often the dreamer will "fix" on one aspect of the dream that has a particular charge, and will overlook other clues and important messages.)

The basic story line of this dream is that Candy has her worst fear come true and lives through it without ill effects. Here are some notes about the dream:

- She has much more control than she realizes since she is seated in the control cabin along with the pilot.
- The jet, a type of business transportation with which Candy is not comfortable, likely represents some aspect of her work life which others consider "normal" but which seems dangerous or overwhelming to her.
- The plane crash is a life-or-death issue. Some part of Candy was facing either issues of financial survival, or questions about where her life was going, possibly both.
- Candy lives through the crash without harm. Even if her worst fears came true, and she "lost everything" she would actually be all right.

As it turned out, Candy was working for a rather high-powered but unscrupulous man. She was involved in exciting but overwhelming business practices which she personally doubted could go on much longer. However, she was terrified of being without financial support. She didn't know what to do for herself (she was at the controls but wasn't taking them). I pointed out to her that even if she "crashed," her dream was indicating that it would not really damage her after all. She expressed a kind of "aha!" She was, she told me, continually stewing about her financial situation and her desire to get out of the business she was in. Although the dream felt like a nightmare, it's message was rather an encouraging one. About six months later Candy left her job and found a more suitable position for herself where she could flourish financially and relax emotionally.

Characters and Setting

When you look for symbols in your dream, be sure to make note of the other characters, and the setting in which the dream takes place. Where are you? And who is there? The other people, (or creatures) in your dream are strong identifiers of meaning. Often people will appear in dreams representing themselves. For example, if you dream of making love with your spouse who is out of town and whom you miss very much, it is extremely likely that you can take the meaning of that dream literally. Often though, dreams will offer you such creative and minutely detailed characters that you will need to write a description of the character before you are able to identify who is being represented. A good red flag with regard to characters is this: if the person in the dream is someone you have never met, or don't know in waking life, someone who is deceased, or someone you haven't seen in years, (or if the character is a talking dog or other magical being), then that character is likely representing someone else, or some part of you, in your waking life.

Here is a dream I had a few years ago in which a television character and I were the only characters. In such a case, it is necessary to go over the *qualities* of the character in order to identify who or what is being represented symbolically.

> *I am waiting in line at a movie theater with MacGiver,*
> *the television character from the action series with*
> *the same name. I am very fond of him, very attracted*
> *to him, and feel a strong rush of affection toward him.*

I wondered who MacGiver represented in this dream. Since he is a fictional character, I knew the representation was symbolic. And, although I enjoy the acting of the young man who plays that part on the television series, I am not romantically attracted to him. Furthermore, I was in a very happy relationship at the time of this dream, and usually had romantic dreams only about my partner. I found it odd that this dream should be an exception. I generated a description of MacGiver to try and identify him in my waking life.

I asked myself the following question: "Who is MacGiver to me, what qualities do I personally associate with that character?" He is smart, and a real survivor who doesn't take a lot of credit for all the miraculous things he does. He's low-key and likeable. You may already have spotted my other big clue. The name MacGiver was spelled differently than it is actually spelled in the series. Since divergence from normal reality is always intentional in dreams, I noted this and set it to one side to decode in the interpretation later. Then I asked myself: "Who does this remind me of?"

It was obvious to me that the character reminded me of my boyfriend at that time, whom I would describe in exactly those terms. He had a tremendous knack for figuring out creative ways to handle tough situations. Then I returned to the spelling of the name MacGiver as a clue to meaning. I had to laugh as I studied it. The day preceding the dream, my boyfriend had given me a Macintosh computer to help me in completing my doctoral dissertation. I was feeling such love and attraction in my dream for "Mac-Giver!" My dreammaker had found a character who combined the sort of self-effacing heroism that fit my partner, and had also given him a name that symbolized my gratitude for the computer.

This style of combining visual symbolism with word-pun clues is extremely common in dreams. It can be a great help in deciphering them, and it never fails to delight dreamers who come to appreciate the striking level of creativity and humor within their own minds.

When you are working with a dream, if you generate a description of a character and it doesn't ring a bell with you, just move on to the next part of the dream. By the time you have described the actions, feelings, and symbols you will often find that a mystery character has spontaneously fallen into place and is revealed as the perfect representation of the person being depicted.

The characters, setting, and objects will often convey the context (or topic) of the dream.

If you dream about people from your work place, even though the dream is set in a situation that doesn't make sense to you, you are likely to be dreaming about elements that are present in your work situation. The co-workers are there because the context of the dream is your work life. There are exceptions to this of course, since the challenges of work and family life tend to overlap. However objects, items, papers, and people from work settings tend to be clues that your dream is work-related.

Sometimes too, a co-worker will be "borrowed" to play a part in a dream because of a quality they represent to you. Here is the dream of a bright and sensitive young man named Nash:

> *I am shoveling a rock pile with Steve, a guy from work. Steve wants to dig out the rock pile from the bottom, but I just know that isn't a good idea. I try to tell him not to tackle the pile that way, but he tells me I'm chicken and he goes ahead. Before we know it, the pile has turned into a mini-avalanche and Steve is buried. I start trying to dig him out. I am scared for him, but mostly I think he was kind of stupid to go about it that way.*

Nash's description of Steve is that he is aggressive and always seems to get his way. Nash confided that he often tells himself he should be more like Steve; more brash and force-ful. He has a tendency to compare himself to Steve, and judge himself as being weak and too sensitive. I knew then that Nash's dreammaker was allowing him to see that the brash way is not always the superior way to "tackle" a project. Nash was more sensitive and (therefore more perceptive), and was able to "just know" a certain approach wasn't a good idea. He was left in the position of having to rescue Steve, thinking to himself that Steve was "kind of stupid."

One of the beauties of dreams is that they are not bound by conscious judgments, and can let us in on a perspective which we might not be aware of when we are blinded by our habitual opinions. In Nash's case, he often considered himself inferior to Steve, but his dreammaker had a more objective opinion, one that Nash benefited from realizing. He was very amused by our deciphering of this dream and was able to curb his tendency to compare himself to others and to be so critical of his own sensitivity.

Setting is the locale where the dream action takes place. Frequent dream settings include the home, the office or work-place, a social gathering, driving or traveling on the road, being in a building of some sort, or the home in which you grew up. The setting is a definite clue to the meaning of the dream, and at times can be "a dead giveaway."

If you dream that you are back in your childhood home, then in all probability you are dreaming about something in your current life that is an echo of your childhood. Many adults continue to have the same nightmare they had when they were little children. This simply means that your subconscious is still experiencing the same fear or issue that was a challenge when you were a child. The "monster" may have a different face now in your waking life, but the psychological dynamic will be roughly the same. (Trouble with authority, handling criticism, trying to win approval through performance, and feeling discounted are typical themes many encounter.)

When you look at the setting of your dream, try to look at it symbolically, rather than literally. Dreams of going back to college may have to do with learning something, or for some, the feeling of going backwards in time to a point when they had less power and were under the authority of others. Dreams of going to a shopping mall or a store often have to do with making choices or searching for something in life that will "fit" your needs. Dreams set in the bedroom of the home, or even in a strange bedroom, may be addressing some aspect of the dreamer's sex life, even when the action involved doesn't seem very sexual.

Let's look at the following dream of a man named Norman who was understandably confused by its imagery.

> *I go up to bed and my wife Nita is on the bed grading papers. I bring in my taxes and spread them out on the bed as well. We don't say anything to each other—just do our paperwork. I feel very anxious though.*

The bedroom **setting** is our first clue. The **action metaphor** of Norman and his wife *lying on the bed* is a pretty big clue that the context of the dream is the intimate side of their marriage. Norman's anxiety is exaggerated and disproportionate for the plot of the dream, and of course the **feelings** involved give us a hint of the dynamic being addressed here. Under the circumstances, it would be logical for Norman to be bored perhaps, but anxious? However, we see that his wife is *grading papers*, which is a **symbol** for *evaluation and judgement of performance*. Norman reacts by bringing in his taxes, and *covering up the bed* with them.

Lets look at language of the dream. The context, revealed by the setting and symbols (the bedroom and the bed) appears to be about the marital relations of Norman and Nita. Norman's emotions given us a clue to the issue or dynamic being expressed: anxiety. Norman is sitting on the bed with his wife *feeling anxious about something.* Nita is grading papers, (evaluating and judging) something *on the bed.* Norman's reaction to Nita's evaluation is to spread his taxes all over the bed and work on them. The taxes might be symbolic of fatigue, "feeling taxed," or of business and financial concerns having to do with the loss of assets. By checking with Norman about these symbols and his associations to them, we were able to get a good understanding of their significance.

Norman and Nita had settled into a routine of avoiding intimate relations. Norman had thought to himself that this was due to his busyness and work headaches. However, the dream revealed that the real issue was his anxiety about being "graded" by Nita. He covered up by claiming he was tired, "taxed" from work. His anxiety over their situation was a hint that he was uncomfortable with this arrangement, but was fearful of changing it. I encouraged Norman to consider how he wanted to use the insight from his dream. It is wise to remember that dreams are trying to help the dreamer by shedding light on things. It is not necessary, however, to burst into action, or to judge yourself for what you do or choose not to do with your dream discoveries.

Insights from dreams give you a greater understanding. What you decide to do with those insights is a matter of personal choice.

As we saw earlier, the **setting** of a dream is an excellent clue to the area of life the dream is about. For instance, if your dream takes place in the lobby of a bank, you may be getting a look at some of your concerns about your financial situation. Or if you dream of selecting clothes during a frantic half-price sale at a shopping mall, your dreammaker may be showing you how confusing you are finding the pressure to make a choice of "attire" or identity.

Your car is often a symbol for your identity in life—your predominant role.

If you are in your car during your dream, or driving any vehicle, it is frequently the case that the dream is dealing with your identity. People changing jobs often dream of getting into their car and finding that it is not their "usual" vehicle. Pregnant women sometimes dream of driving a larger car than is normal for them, such as a truck or bus, and of finding it awkward to manage. Anyone taking on a larger professional identity than usual may find themselves dreaming of driving a "larger" vehicle as well. Someone dreaming of driving a horse and buggy down a busy freeway with speeding drivers swerving around him may be dealing with feelings of not being "with the times," or of being dangerously out of date. As I tackled the enormous paperwork involved with finishing my doctoral work in psychology, I often dreamed of driving my car up extremely steep hills, and of feeling afraid that my car wouldn't have the power to get to the top.

A house may be a symbol for the self.

If your dream is set in a house which is not known to you in your waking life, you will need to describe it for yourself, and then identify the meaning from your description. Many dream analysts believe that the house is the symbol for the self and is sometimes symbolic of the physical body. If the house is compartmentalized, then the dreamer may have distinct divisions or compartments to the personality. Often a split between emotions and rational thinking will be depicted by a divided dream house. If the house has so many windows that you feel exposed and vulnerable inside, and any passerby can see in at any time, it is likely that you feel exposed in you waking life. (As with any generalization, these thoughts need to be "tried on" to see if they fit for you.)

Look for similarities between the description of the house, its qualities, and some area of your waking life. If you are presently looking for a career change, and you dream of driving through different neighborhoods to see where you want to "live," the dream is likely acting out your internal search for a place where you feel you will belong. Many times people facing a choice of some kind will dream of looking for a place to live, and of entering a possible home only to find it disgusting or totally unsuitable. These dreams can be valuable guides about choices the dreamer would be wise to avoid.

Sometimes the setting of a dream will be in fantasy-land. You may dream of floating through a rainbow, sitting on a cloud, or even of appearing in a *Star Trek* episode. Just take the setting and describe it back to yourself. Take whatever the dream offers you, and assume that it is ideal for depicting the exact meaning the dreammaker is trying convey.

Sometimes we forget to take note of a setting because we take it for granted, or because it doesn't seem important. Remember, any dream can be set *anywhere*; the exact setting for your dream was selected intentionally because it is representative of meaning for you.

Although characters and setting are symbolic, many **symbols** are objects or things that appear in dreams as part of the story line or action. These don't always make logical sense, but they will when you describe them to yourself and check that description for what it reminds you of in your waking life. Incongruities, and "strange" things, are wonderful clues to meaning. For example, here the a dream of a young girl named Linda from a struggling period in her education.

> *I am trying to get my books open to study but they are locked. I am suddenly scared. If I can't get into them in time, I won't pass the test. I get a hammer and try to break the locks. I hit them and they turn into rotten eggs and run all over everything. I think "Rotten eggs? How childish."*

Since Linda was experiencing anxiety and frustration about her studies at this time, we were safe in assuming that the apparent context of her dream was indeed her education. The lock represented her challenge in working with material that was new and frightening to her. She was afraid that she might not be able to "get into it" in time to pass her test. Her attempt to solve the situation though, to "hammer" through the locks resulted in the locks changing into rotten eggs which ran all over and spoiled everything. Linda's description of *rotten eggs* was that they were something children foolishly threw to spoil things. She thought to herself in the dream: "rotten eggs, how childish." This was the dreammaker's way of telling Linda that her attempt to hammer her way into the material was childish, and would have the opposite result of the one she wanted. Linda decided to get some tutoring to help her with the unknown portions of her material, and to approach the situation with a more "mature," and less panicky style of learning. It is likely that her very attempts to *force* herself to master material she found confusing were inhibiting her ability to comprehend aspects of it which were accessible to her.

Strange or "weird" dream events are a real gift to interpretation— don't judge them, be grateful!

It is unfortunate that dream studies are not more available to people early in life. There seems to be a level of exploration that can only be enjoyed by deciding to accept the oddities of the dream realm. Some people find the apparent bizarreness of their symbols to be so exotic that they actually discount any meaning their dream might have. It seems so "weird" that they dismiss it as indigestion or as just a random event. While some dreams *are* more significant than others, they are never random, nor are the pieces or actions that comprise them. Whatever you are examining within your dream, keep in mind that it holds meaning for you, and that its appearance and placement are no accident.

If you balance this assumption with common sense, and put reasonable effort into understanding dream language, you will reap great rewards without becoming compulsively driven toward perfect analysis. As with incongruities and differences, bizarre and magical elements also are great clues to meaning. In fact, such elements often make the interpretation much more accessible. Let's look at the dream a student named Ted had when his roommate from college planned to come home with him for a visit during school break.

> *I arrive home with Chris, my college roommate, and find that our house isn't the same. It is really ramshackle and awful. The porch is all rotten and horrible; it looks like hillbillies live there. Then I go in and introduce Chris around, and all my family is dressed like the Beverly Hillbillies. They are missing teeth and everything. I am so embarrassed, because Chris comes from a really rich family. I am sorry I invited him to join me for vacation, but he doesn't seem to notice anything wrong. He is friendly with everybody, and everybody but me is having a great time. Then a funny thing happens. I go in the bathroom and notice sparkles in the soap dish. Then we have dinner, and there are sparkles at everyone's plate. Every member of the family has these sparkles at their place. I pick one up, and see that it is a diamond. There are diamonds everywhere, all through the house, especially around my family.*

In Ted's dream the house of his family looked shabby and horrible, but only to him, not to the dream characters. He felt critical and horribly embarrassed about his family and their "hillbilly" ways, but his rich friend Chris was not offended and didn't seem to see anything wrong. This suggests that the ramshackle quality of the house was in *Ted's perspective*, not anyone else's. (This is a case where the dream reflects back a viewpoint which is outside of the dreamer's conscious perspective—yet which he would benefit from seeing.)

The context of the dream is indeed Ted's family life, as revealed by the setting. The issue addressed in the dream is revealed by Ted's feelings; embarrassment about bringing a wealthy friend home to visit his more "humble" family.

Let's look at the action of the dream. The family gets along well with Chris, and he with them. This is a case where the dreamer's fears don't match what actually occurs. Dreams of a dreaded event that turns out surprisingly well are usually signals that the level of worry being indulged in is inappropriate and unnecessary.

The most fascinating symbol of this dream is, of course, the diamonds. Ted's dreammaker lets him wonder for a while about all the "sparkles" in the house, before he picks one up and recognizes it as a diamond. Ted described a diamond as valuable, indestructible, and permanent. "Something very precious" that people give to each other out of love. Ted was worried that his family home would look "ramshackle" to his rich college friend, but Ted's dreammaker was reminding him that his home and family had "diamonds all over the place." Ted's family home was full of the precious, indestructible value of love.

Symbols are your dreammaker's way of representing something to you in a novel or unusual way that highlights the quality of what is depicted. Often a symbol will represent the particular quality with a poetic artistry that is quite poignant, as in Ted's dream.

Consider for example, what this dream would have been like if there had been no diamonds in the house, but instead Ted's father had given a mini-lecture at the dinner table saying, "Ted's ashamed of our middle class house, but he's forgotten what good people we really are." The message of the dream would have been similar, but Ted would not have carried with him the *emotional* impact of recognizing the diamonds, and the haunting beauty of the "sparkles" all over the family home.

The more you work with dreams the more appreciation you will gain for the fascinating language which can convey both ideas and emotions with the same image.

Learning common symbols can be a good short-cut, but always double-check your personal associations to get the accurate meaning.

When describing symbols for yourself or your dream group, if you don't know what to make of an object, start with what the item means to you. Frequently, your association will be slightly different from the everyday one, or will reveal an important slant that you need to be aware of. In the previous example, another dreamer might have considered diamonds to be "bad investments which don't allow you to profit much for your effort." It was Ted's description that counted and revealed meaning. Just as it is your description of an object or setting that matters in understanding your own dream.

A word of caution here. Most of us assume that our understanding of the world *is* the general consensus. If black stockings symbolize prostitution to you, it doesn't mean that the same association will be made by another dreamer. If you are helping someone else with a dream, don't assume that *your* meaning for a symbol is their meaning. You may offend them, or even worse, you may convince them of an interpretation that is based on your associations. This will be less accurate, since their dreammaker is generating material out of *their understanding of the world.*

When in a dream group, or working with a friend, you may want to get a feel for how different associations are by playing this game:

> Pick something a little unusual, like "red patent-leather shoes" and go around the group asking each person to share what red patent leather shoes are. It is not adequate to say, "I agree with what Mary said." Each person must generate a description for themselves. You may get to some interesting material by asking further, "What kind of person wears red patent-leather shoes?" My own answer would be: "Red patent-leather shoes are worn by little girls who would rather be wearing sneakers or moccasins, but whose mommies are making them dress up."

The description that "pops out of you" and is personal (but feels universal) is the one you want. It isn't necessary, unless you feel suspicious, to delve for deep psychological symbolism or abstract connections. The connection you want is the personal one. It will be a perfect fit for you, and it will apply beautifully to your current life situation.

If someone tries to "help you out" by informing you that dreams of fire are always about sexual repression, thank them for their input, but don't necessarily believe them. Instead, hold that as *one* possibility, and ask yourself some questions about the quality of the symbol to arrive at your own connections. What was the fire like? Describe it for yourself. Was it powerful and all-consuming, but not scary? Was it exciting? Did you want to get it burning brighter, or were you scared out of your wits and running to call the fire department? What it was *like* for you, along with the context of the dream will help you discover the meaning it holds.

I have a friend who is one of the most forceful and dynamic women I have ever met. Beautiful, bright, fast-talking and aggressive, she has the kind of drive that makes one want to try mega-vitamins. She now runs her own business, but prior to that she worked at a job that bored her and failed to challenge or reward her adequately. She told me that during that time she repeatedly dreamed of a fire that was powerful and beautiful but confined. It wasn't difficult to recognize that the fire was *her*, her spirit, ambition, and personal power. When she branched out on her own she no longer had the fire dreams, perhaps because that part of herself was allowed to flourish in her waking reality.

Uncovering Your Dream's Meaning

Here is an overview of the basic steps for uncovering your dream's meaning. These elements will be covered in detail in the next chapter:

1. Record the dream:
   Use simple language and write in present tense. Note your thoughts and feelings during the dream. (I see my sister. I feel angry.) If the dream is rather long, break the action into scenes, and write them in paragraphs.
2. Underline or note:
   - Action Metaphors (fought, climbed, struggled, got lost).
   - Exaggerated Feelings. How you felt during the dream, or what it was like for you to go through the action. (I watched my house burn down, *and I was relieved.*)
   - Symbols (characters, setting, objects).
3. Generate a description of the action-metaphors, symbols, and feelings. Repeat the description to yourself, or if you are working with others, have someone repeat the

description to you. What does this remind you of in your waking life? If you have generated the description carefully, you will be startled by the connections you see to your waking life. If you have a long dream, take it scene by scene, generating a description for each scene. Finish making all your descriptions, then begin checking for connections.

Some people like to use a colored high-lighter to mark the action, symbols, and feelings in their dream record. Others have better luck by underlining, and then writing a description after the dream record. The method you use is up to you. As you make a habit of recording your dreams and examining them, you will naturally discover the approach that works best for you. The idea is to train yourself to attend to the action, feelings, and symbols in the dream, to lift them out of the dream itself and then identify their connections to your waking life.

Other Dream Clues

In addition to action metaphors, exaggerated feelings, and symbols, dreams sometimes offer us even stronger clues to meaning.

Quotes and direct comments are clues to meaning

Any time you make a direct comment to someone in a dream, particularly if conversation is minimal in the rest of the action, you have an interesting clue. For example, if you confront a loved one, and say "I'm not going to put up with this anymore," you have an excellent thread of feeling and insight to trace back to your waking reality. Sometimes self-talk offers a literal connection to the waking context; you may indeed be dreaming about that loved one, and something they've been putting over on you. Or you may be expressing a thought that is directed toward someone you dare not visualize, even in a dream. Go through the dream normally, and then ask yourself: Where in life am I feeling: *I'm not going to put up with this anymore?* Don't overlook the possibility that the dreammaker may be using the loved one to represent a quality of yourself.

Brief dreams in which someone appears, tells you something, and leaves often have delightful and rather direct insights to offer. I call these **advice dreams**, and depending upon the content, you may want to take them rather literally. In one of my favorite **advice dreams**, my grandmother appeared to me, said: "quit worrying so much, just do the best you can," and left. I was amused and touched that my dreammaker had selected one of the champion advise-givers of all time to pass on this little gem. Needless to say, if someone appears to you in a dream and gives you advice that is harmful, such as "Pull out all your hair," you would not want to follow that recommendation. Use common sense with dreams, just as you would if a friend or acquaintance made a suggestion to you. Just because it comes to you in a dream doesn't make advice infallible; although the tendency is going to be for your advice dreams to benefit you. Another favorite advice dream came to me about a year after the end of a romantic relationship I had been particularly sad to lose.

> *I am driving a new convertible. With me is Jake (an old boyfriend). He is riding in the passenger seat. He turns to me and says, "You can let me out anywhere, you know. You don't have to take me with you all the time anymore."*

This dream was giving me very sound advice indeed. I had continued to grieve over this relationship and to doubt myself long after it was time to "let go" of my memories. Driving a new sporty convertible suggested that my ability to change and "convert" experiences into positive lessons was a strong advantage to me. Obviously, Jake telling me to "drop him off anywhere" was my dreammaker's way of letting me know I was really free. Because of this dream I was able to retrieve that "OK, now I'm really alive" feeling which is the signal of a return to wholeness. It is interesting to note that this dream came to me on the anniversary of our breakup. It is quite common for anniversary dreams to take place, even several years after the event. Don't be dismayed if you dream of a sad episode on the anniversary of its occurrence. This doesn't mean that you have not dealt with the issue or made progress after so much time. Rather, it seems that our emotional natures mark time with extraordinary recall. You may be unaware of the anniversary until the dream points it out to you. Be gentle with your painful feelings, and acknowledge the wisdom of your dreammaker in sketching again the outlines of your pivotal experiences. Many therapists recommend that on such "emotional anniversaries" you take extra care by doing something special to nourish or nurture yourself. Certainly the more accepting and gentle we are with our feelings, the more able we are to learn from them and allow the natural course of healing to unfold.

Self-talk dreams are often quite powerful too, and their meaning can be rather direct. These dreams typically have little dialog, but at some point you think to yourself, "I'm not going to put myself down anymore," or "I don't have anything to be ashamed of," or "This is what I really want to do." Many times the context of the dream is a literal representation of the waking context the dream is addressing. Here is an example:

> *I buy some dessert from a deli counter. I am shocked to find that the piece of cake I bought cost me $19.00. I sit down to eat it, and find it is stale and unappealing. I think to myself: "I'm not going to eat deserts anymore. The cost is too high."*

This dream came to me at a time when I was having difficulties with fatigue. I never seemed to have enough energy to accomplish the things I wanted to do. I had been considering making an appointment with a physician for a physical, but I hesitated to do so since my intuition told me I would, as always, be told that there was nothing wrong with me. I was amused by the rather blunt way my dreammaker was telling me that I could not "afford" to indulge my sweet tooth. The fact that the dessert was stale and unappealing was yet another level of information that sugar was not fuel that my body could use. I eventually heeded the advise of this dream, and found that altering my diet helped me to feel more energetic than I had ever thought possible.

Other self-talk dreams may use more metaphoric action and symbolism in the setting. However, in the majority of cases the setting and content which you comment about will be closely aligned with your waking reality. In most cases the comment you make to yourself will be important to your waking reality, so whenever you recall that you said something to yourself in a dream make a special effort to record and decipher it.

Dream puns are another excellent clue to meaning. The dreammaker in each of us tends to be creative, poetic, and artistic. Many people cannot imagine how such intricate and profound dreams can have been created within their own minds. Dream puns are another example of the artistry and humor with which our dreams are woven. A friend of mine recently had the following dream:

> I am in a second-hand store and I see a new toy train. I go pick it up. It's really neat. Shiny and clever. I like it a lot.

When I asked my friend if he had recently begun toying with a new train of thought, he burst out laughing and shared with me that he was indeed exploring a new business idea. Unlike some of his previous ideas, which he had gotten "second hand," this was an original idea that he found "neat" and "clever."

When working with a dream, don't be afraid to set it on its ear and look for dream puns. Here is a dream Pat, a horse-rancher, had when considering a fairly simple horse-breeding arrangement.

> I get the semen for breeding the horse by artificial insemination. Instead of the usual way, it comes in a little cake which will be fed to the horse later. On the way to where I am going I start nibbling on the cake. Pretty soon I notice that I have eaten practically the whole thing. Now, I think, I'll have to go get some more. I wonder if I have enough money for another cake.

As she explained to me, breeding a horse by artificial insemination is both simple and tricky. Because of the very artificial procedure, sometimes the mare doesn't "settle" and become pregnant. I asked Pat if there was any chance that she was overestimating how simple the arrangement was going to be, because, in her dream, she was expecting it to be "a piece of cake!" She agreed with me, and did me one better by noting: "I guess I thought I would be able to *have my cake and eat it too."*

Dream puns are quite common, and the more you allow yourself to be on the lookout for them, the more you will be able to spot. It is sometimes easier to spot the puns in someone else's dream; they can be so obvious you burst out laughing when you hear the dream. Always be sensitive to the dreamer's feelings, and to the intimate nature of the material that is dealt with in dreams. Sometimes you will have to "lay low" with what you see in a dream, if your intention is to help another dreamer to uncover meaning for themselves. As with any area of friendship and psychological support use gentleness, respect, and caring as your guidelines for interaction.

Chapter 5

The 5-Step Technique

In working with the dreams of students and clients, I have identified 5 "check-points" that help the dreamer get to the heart of what the dream is trying to communicate. I recommend these steps to get you started in working with dreams that do not have obvious meaning to you, or where only part of the meaning is clear. As you become more experienced, feel free to move on from these steps; they are not meant to be the only route you can take.

There is a saying in Great Britain: "All roads lead to London." In some sense, with dreamwork all roads will lead you into meaning, but certain areas of inquiry seem more expedient and less confusing than others and require no adherence to a particular school or philosophy. Here is the 5-step method:

1. **Check Your First Impression of the Dream**
2. **Note the Action Metaphors it Contains**
3. **Notice Your Feelings During the Dream**
4. **Notice the Symbols including Characters and Setting**
5. **Check for the "Gift" within the Dream**

Let's go over these steps in detail:

1. Get a First Impression

I call this your first "hit" about what a dream is addressing. Don't grab onto a symbol or go off on a tangent about any portion of the dream yet. Rather, take a mental step back and view it as if it were a movie or a painting. If a friend asked you about a movie you'd just seen and you could only say 3 or 4 words about it, you would move automatically into "impression shorthand." That is, you might say, "Scary, Elm Street with a love story." Or, "Western re-run with new actors." Or "tragedy that leaves you drained." "Story of suffering." Or "The underdog who wins against all odds." Or "Love gone wrong."

You get the idea. If you are sharing the dream with others, ask them for their first impression too. Not a full interpretation, just a first impression. Many newcomers jump in and try to make a link with waking reality at this step, with disastrous and nonsensical results. This is not the point at which to ask: "Are you considering having an affair?" This is the moment to *observe* the mood of the dream, and say: "It seems to be about a longing for intimacy." If everyone in the group sees the same thing, you are likely on target.

This **first impression** will give you a good start on working with the dream, and will serve as a kind of map of the territory you are about to explore. It will also prevent you from making the typical mistake of turning off your mind's capacity to recognize meaning by saying right off the bat: "I don't know what this dream means, it is meaningless to me." It is *terribly* hard to engage your capacity to understand something right after you have instructed your brain not to understand. While it is fairly natural not to understand the dream when you first look at it, simply note the thing about it that does strike you. It may be about confusion, frustration, challenges, or fear. Perhaps the overall quality of the dream may strike you as noteworthy. Even if you are dealing with a dream fragment about the color red, note your overall impression, don't take it for granted that red is a frightening color to everyone - it isn't. Note that red reminds you of blood and injury and thus you are disturbed by the recollection of this fragment. In such a case your first impression would be of something disturbing. That's all you need to know at this stage, and it's an excellent start.

2. Note the Action Metaphors

If you are working with a written version of the dream, underline or highlight the action passages. These are moments when you kick down a door, hide in a closet, fly through iron bars, take your dog outside, or look for a new house, etc. When you have isolated the action passages, look at their metaphoric possibilities. If you are sharing your dream with others orally, ask someone to jot down the action-metaphors so that the connections are not lost. For example, taking a seat on the toilet, looking up and finding you are in the middle of a busy office rather than in a lavatory would be a bit of action. Translated into metaphor the action might reflect attempting to do something very private, possibly embarrassing and finding yourself exposed in public. (Deeper meaning would be revealed by the dreamer's exact feelings about this, such as humiliation, frustration at lack of privacy, or fear of what others might think.) These action metaphors can be used to expand on your first impression, and begin to firm up your suspicions about the dream's meaning.

The action is generally the "story" of the dream, such as being a victim, needing to defend yourself, being exploited, trying to heal someone, or looking for love. Once you have examined the actions and revealed their metaphoric implications you are well on your way to a good interpretation. At this stage dreamers may begin to feel a certain excitement of recognition because they are no longer trapped in the appearance of the dream, but are experiencing the satisfaction of uncovering an emotional translation for the action. When you begin to work with meaning rather than appearance, everything about the dream starts to become exciting and empowering. You may notice a quickening sensation, and a sense of momentum building as things begin to make sense to your conscious mind. Forging this connection between the dreammaker (or subconscious) and your conscious mind is a very uplifting and liberating experience. The more often this occurs, the more resources you are free to use from within this "connected zone" at any time.

3. Notice Your Feelings

For many people, attending to their feelings in dreams is the toughest discipline of all to master. You may have to *force* yourself to look for your feelings in the dream until it becomes a habit. It is easy for most of us to overlook our feelings about the action, or to take those feelings for granted and disregard them as part of the dream. Remember, your reactions to the "story" are possibly the *most important part* of the story.

If you are working with a written record or with your dream journal, be sure to record and underline your emotions. When sharing the dream, be sure to include your feelings in your description so that others can incorporate them into their analysis. Without knowing the feelings involved, it is difficult to know whether seeing the ghost of your dead grandmother was a hideous nightmare or a spiritually uplifting experience of love and connection. Although emotions in dreams are often exaggerated, they tend to parallel your actual feelings about the waking life situation being addressed. While the objects and people in your dreams may be symbolic, and actions as we just discussed are often metaphorical, emotions you experience in dreams tend to be fairly consonant with your waking emotions. A scary situation in a dream can be used to inquire: Where in my waking life do I feel this way? Who makes me feel used, or humiliated in waking life?

Therapists often trace a present day emotion back to its origin by using what is called an "affective bridge." They keep asking the client, "when was the first time you remember feeling this way?" In a sense, the emotion itself acts as a kind of memory tracer which can be followed back through time to its origin so that the individual can perhaps process the initial incident that gave rise to the recurring emotion. Similarly, the emotion you have in a dream can be used as a reminder, a marker to point you towards the situation or issue in your waking life where you have similar feelings.

Keep in mind that the emotions in your dream will likely be much stronger and more dramatic than you experience them in your waking life. You may even have been suppressing a bit of your feelings in waking life, particularly if the feelings are what we would label as negative. It may help you to close your eyes and step back into the dream mentally for a few moments to get a "taste" of the feelings again. Noticing your feelings is particularly important during dream action that seems bizarre and inexplicable. Often events in dreams will take a turn that may seem out of context with the overall action, and this can prove a challenge unless you can utilize your recall of emotion to guide your inquiry.

One woman in our group dreamed of going to a dance in the basement of her girlhood church and then of seeing teenage boys shooting-up heroine in the hallway. This action didn't remind her of anything at first, and frankly the group was puzzled by it. It was only when we asked her about her feelings that she began to recognize the dream was about someone in her life who was repeatedly doing something harmful under the auspices of recreational, and even spiritual reasons.

At first when we asked about her feelings, she explained that she was merely a witness to the action and didn't feel like a participant in the dream. This "observer" sensation in dreams is not uncommon and is in itself a clue, since it reflects the waking life "position" of the dreamer to the situation or context. (How many times have you felt like you were watching the events of your life rather than participating in them? How many times have you watched yourself make a mistake, or change your direction and felt that you were both the actor and the observer of your life? Particularly with regard to destructive or frightening events, we tend to watch our marriages disintegrate, or our children act out with a sense of helplessness.) In the case of this woman, it was her sense of being a helpless witness to harmful waste and self-delusion that triggered her awareness of the dream's meaning.

After identifying your feelings and linking them to the waking life situation that strikes a similar emotional cord you will be on the way to a strong interpretation. In general it is the emotions in a dream which clinch the interpretation. However, some of us don't seem to recall strong feelings; either they fade rapidly, or they don't seem to be a big part of the dream. Don't worry if that is the case for you. Just apply yourself to remembering what feelings you can and note them for later use in your overall interpretation.

4. Note the Symbols (Including Characters and Setting)

Historically dream symbolism has been given a lot of press. There is something fascinating about the notion that objects in dreams represent things symbolically. Because we are a society that uses language and numbers as representations for meaning, we tend to have great faith in the notion of symbolism.

Many scholars have written masses of material about symbols and this tends to be the one idea people share about dreamwork: that is, that dream objects represent things other than what they appear to be.

Consider your personal connection to your dream's image. If you have none, then consider general associations that are common to everyone.

The most pragmatic approach to decoding symbols is to search for the dreamer's association to the symbol. (A rose means true love to some people, and mental illness to others. What determines the interpretation is *what it means to the dreamer.*) As with the other steps, record and underline the symbols. Look at the setting, the buildings, the characters, and any objects you pick up or look at, or look for. It may be confusing at first to look for symbols, since almost anything might be symbolic, but by quickly underlining the people, the place, and the objects involved you will have a good start.

Once you have underlined the symbols, go through them one by one and see if you can recognize the clues they represent to meaning. This procedure need not be terribly deep or infused with Freudian implications. For example, if some of the characters in the dream are colleagues from work, the dream is *highly likely* to have something to do with work issues. The use of colleagues in dreams seems to be standard shorthand for work-related dreams. Even if the action and setting take place away from the office, if you have a co-worker with you in the river raft, or on safari, then you are likely having a work-related dream.

The second short-cut to know about dream characters is that often relatives such as cousins, parents, or grandparents are used when the dream is dealing with issues or patterns that originated in your family system. Don't be afraid of simple explanations. They are often correct.

It is not unusual to repeatedly dream of an old friend, even someone who is now dead, despite the fact that they are no longer part of your waking life. When this happens, here are some good questions to ask yourself to determine why your dreammaker is using this person so often when creating your dreams.

1. What was going on in your life when this person was around?

   You may have felt like a victim in those days, and be having a similar experience now, even though you have essentially outgrown that pattern. Or, you may be selling out to the boss the way you compromised in your marriage. People are often used as emotional snapshots of moments of feeling in life. It may help you find your association to a character by thinking of him or her as a portrait of your feelings at the time that you knew him or her.

2. What overall characteristic do you associate with them?

Try to define it in one word or one phrase. Assertive? Bossy? A Brown-Noser? A Company Man? The Class Clown? A User? A Temptress? This is particularly important if a person who is no longer in your waking life is *constantly* showing up in your dreams. It is almost certain that this person has come to represent a particular quality or characteristic in your subconscious, perhaps one that you wrestle with in yourself, or do not allow out to see the light of day. It is also possible that this person has a characteristic in common with someone in your waking life and your dreammaker is illustrating the similarity that you fail to notice consciously.

3. After deciding on a descriptive phrase or adjective to define the character, ask yourself "Who in my life, or what part of myself is like this?"

If after defining your association to the character you still do not have a connection to your waking life, it may be that the character is representing the quality of something missing from your life. For example, one woman I worked with had a girlhood friend in boarding school who had taught her things about joy, humor and being herself that she carried with her for the rest of her life. As an adult she missed the amazing closeness she'd had with this girl, and longed for the camaraderie they'd shared as teenagers. During those times, she would again dream of her dear friend, and they would embark on new adventures together in their same spirited way. The day following such a dream she would miss her friend more acutely than ever, and wonder about its possible meaning.

In my opinion, she had these dreams for two reasons: First, she needed this kind of friendship, craved it, and couldn't seem to find it again in her waking life, so her dreammaker helped provide a kind of balance by creating episodes of friendship for her in dreams. (We have all dreamed of finding our one true love and spending a blissful night with him or her.) Secondly, her dreammaker was showing her that the essence of this friendship and joy resides in *her* and is always with her. While it is a privilege to have someone to love, it is not necessary to have that person in order to be *loving*. It is all too easy to attribute emotions that are *ignited or catalyzed* by another as having their origin in the other. Dreams frequently attempt to show us that our most precious feelings are always available within us; *that we are virtually inexhaustible reservoirs of feeling* despite the fact that we sometimes turn off the faucet when someone dear leaves our life, and pretend to ourselves that love or humor or security went with them.

5. Check for "The Gift"

I believe that dreams are always working to bring us closer to health, wholeness and greater development as individuals. To this end, they often provide advice, insights, and new perspectives on old questions *embedded within the action of the dream.* It took me several years of work with the dreams of students before I recognized this as a uniform feature of dreams. It is entirely possible to arrive at a successful and satisfying interpretation of a dream without recognizing the most magical and powerful element it contains. This extra element, this magical note of wisdom is "the Gift."

Often the Gift will be noted by the dreamer's thoughts during the action. I recently dreamed of flying through an empty house and coming up against a wall. I thought that if I just believed I could move through the wall, then I would. This thought was immediately followed by the wall becoming permeable, and my sliding through it to the other side. In addition to the other meaningful aspects this dream contained, this moment was a gift to me because it served to remind me how many of the barriers in my life could be surmounted or dissolved if I would simply believe in my power to move through them. I hold this as a truth in my experience, yet like most human beings, I sometimes become convinced by apparent limitations without considering whether it is actually *necessary* to be held back by them. The Gift in your dreams will frequently be a hint that it is time to reexamine your assumptions.

Look for the Gift in some of your comments during the dream. One dreamer announced to the other characters that he wasn't going to struggle up the side of a mountain because he'd once been told to. This man had decided to pursue a calmer, more personally meaningful life for himself than the traditional "climb to the top."

A young woman who was afraid of being swept away by the rush of emotions that accompanied a romantic break up dreamed she was holding on to rocky crags while the tide rose beneath her and threatened to drown her. Suddenly though, she "remembered" that if she believed in her capacity to survive, she would be all right. She calmed herself and the tide began to ebb.

Direct quotes in dreams can be astonishingly profound, and are often an area to examine when looking for the Gift. It is particularly difficult for most people to recognize these comments when they are of a strikingly positive nature. For example, one woman went through a great many adventures in one dream, exploring, sleuthing, and crossing the countryside on her own. During one section, she found herself crossing swords with an adversary, and executing amazing thrusts and parries against her opponent. The thought came to her: *"I am really good at this. I should do this more often."*

During our work with the dream, it was easy to become caught up in the action adventure, which had to do with bringing all her talents and ambitions together into her right livelihood. The Gift though, had to do with the very aggressive action of the sword-fight, and her recognition that she was good at it, and should do it more often. This helped her to make a decision about whether or not to take pre-law as she returned to school. She was soft-spoken, and most of her friends had expressed doubt as to whether she would be able to argue her point of view adequately. However the dream showed her as being a natural when it came to "picking up the sword" (of justice?) and executing very aggressive and defensive moves against an opponent. This is an example of a dream's ability to reflect a more accurate picture of the real you than may be known even to your friends.

The Gift may come in moments of realization within the action as well. Typically a dreamer will recount the action of a dream following a certain logical sequence, and then will experience a "realization" that offers an unexpected twist to events. One woman dreamed of waiting in line at a cafeteria (a place of choices). While waiting in line to get up to the counter and place her order (make her choice) *she realized that the line was going nowhere.* This dream happened to be about her work setting, where she enjoyed working, and hoped to be in line for promotion. However, her dreammaker was well aware that this job was a dead-end for her, and that is why she *realized* the line was going nowhere. In her waking life situation she *was* in fact patiently waiting her turn in a line that was going nowhere. This Gift caused her to begin to explore professional opportunities she had put on the back burner for months, and to reexamine the long term effects of her career choices.

Finally, the gift may appear to you when you look over the entire action of the dream. It is not uncommon to dream repeatedly of your worst fear. For some of us, it has to do with the metaphor of a terrible accident befalling us. For others, it has to do with a theme of betrayal by a loved one. Many of my initial consultations come about because someone finally decides they have to know why they keep dreaming of their worst fear. It is interesting to note however, that in many of these cases, the person is overlooking the entire action of the dream, and is failing to perceive the gift being offered to them.

One woman dreamed that she thought her husband was having an affair. In her dreams she would follow him around consumed with jealousy, and arrange to come home unexpectedly and "catch him in the act." Invariably however, she would find that he was not engaged in an affair at all, but she would still accuse him in a jealous fit, and they would fight. She would end the dream very frightened of losing him.

This woman was wringing her hands when she discussed these dreams, because she believed that a recurring dream was more likely to come true, and she actually thought of them as visions of "Ron" having an affair. It startled her, and stopped our conversation cold when I asked her if he ever *did* have an affair in any of these dreams. The answer was no. We looked at each other for a moment as this sunk in. I said: "So these are very frightening dreams of something really awful that never really happens?" I explained to her that dream action is far from random, it is meaningful in every detail. It would make more sense, in a way, for the plot of these dreams to unfold and reveal a philandering husband, than to go to the trouble of taking a plot twist and have the husband remain innocent while she goes on accusing him. Together, we saw that these dreams were telling her that *fear* was her worst enemy, along with strong doses of obsessive thinking and insecurity.

She had thought of these as infidelity dreams, and had failed even to *register* the fact that the infidelity never occurred. We look at our lives through the lens of our fears unfortunately, and great distortions tend to take place.

This is demonstrated graphically with dreams in which the individual is in a terrible plane crash, (like Candy) and survives without a scratch. Or where someone's house burns down and they are able to extricate their most precious object and emerge unscathed. Many of what people think of as "disaster" dreams are actually "survival" dreams, in which we are shown either the part we play in perpetuating our fears, or that we would certainly survive even if our worst scenario came true. Keep in mind when looking for the Gift that it will almost certainly be something *you don't already know* about a subject or issue you think you know all about!

Putting the Interpretation Together

Simply moving through the 5-Step process will usually be all you need to do to uncover the meaning of a dream. Here is the sequence again:

1. **Check Your First Impression**
2. **Notice the Action Metaphors**
3. **Note Your Feelings**
4. **Note the Symbols (including character and setting)**
5. **Check for The Gift**

But once in a while you may work through the dream and still emerge with only a vague sense of what it concerns. When that happens your next best step is to take separate piece of paper and write down only the five points in the order they appear in the dream.

Jot down the first impression, all action metaphors, feelings, symbols, and what you see as the Gift. Then read the abbreviated version out loud to yourself (or the group) and see how it strikes you. Here is an example using one of the dreams I had while writing this book:

> *I'm lying on the floor somewhere in a class using a book for a pillow. Everyone is lying on the floor listening to a lecture. Someone in the very back of the room says: "The part of yourself you don't love is the part you most want others to love." I sit up and tell the instructor that this is a most critical point, and that it*

has to do with Jung's anima/animus theory, as well as what I refer to as "the abandoned child" dreams. When I sit up, the book remains on top of my head, balanced there like a hat, and the teacher asks me to repeat what I've just said only facing the other students so that they can read my lips.

Here is how the 5 elements read when excerpted from the dream.

I'm lying on the floor using a book for a pillow.

listening to a lecture

"The part of yourself you don't love is the part you most want others to love."

I sit up "a most critical point,"

the book remains on top of my head, repeat what I've just said

only facing the other students so that they can read my lips.

The meaning becomes much easier to glimpse when recorded in this short-hand. Lying on the floor is a passive pose, and I had been taking a rather passive attitude towards the completion of this book. Listening to a lecture is also a passive, student-like pose, and I realized that after 10 years of college, I still secretly identify myself as a student rather than as a teacher. Using the book as a pillow reflects the way that I, like so many writers tend to use the book as an excuse not to do other things: use it to cushion my repose.

The statement from the back of the room which makes me sit up (take a more active position) is an interesting bit of advice. In my case, some of my reluctance to pursue career goals with more aggressiveness stems from a fear of criticism, and indeed, I am very critical of myself. The part of myself I criticize, I tend to shield from others lest they criticize it too, yet I want terribly to have that part loved by others, so that in turn, I can love it more myself. Of course, life doesn't work that way. Only by allowing self-acceptance is confidence in ourselves reflected in the way others respond to us.

There is a wonderful dream pun in my comment "this is a critical point." The dream is *about* my fear of criticism, and it is also a critical point in my growth to move through this particular fear. The dream ends with the teacher asking me to address the class and share this bit of wisdom. I am wearing my book hat, which implies a change of persona: speaking as the teacher/author rather than lying back as a student. The teacher asks me to face the class when I speak so that they can read my lips. This may have to do with the simplicity of my message, and the straightforward and "learnable" approach I take to dreamwork. I am asked to "face" the people who would like to know what I have to share. The Gift in this dream is the statement coming from the back of the room about self-love. None of us can afford to wait for the endorsement we want from others, we must first provide it for ourselves; and then, miraculously that which we thought we needed from others will indeed begin to become part of our experience.

Chapter 6

Typical Symbols and Metaphors

Although I am not in favor of dream dictionaries that make pronouncements such as: "Cows are always symbols of calcium deficiency," there are general tendencies in dream metaphors and symbols which can be used as short-cuts if you use them as broad, general guidelines. Here are some examples.

Pregnancy

If you are trying to become pregnant, a dream of pregnancy may be a trial run of what it will feel like for you, or it might be that your body-mind system has detected the pregnancy before your conscious mind. If you are not of an age or position to become pregnant, then a dream of pregnancy is likely an indication that you are in a situation which is like gestation. You are carrying some kind of new life within you. This may be a book, or a project, or a new life-style. It is quite common for women approaching times of transition to dream of being pregnant. Sometimes this is in reference to the "new self" which is soon to emerge. If you are contemplating a change, such as returning to college, dissolving a marriage, moving to another city, or changing jobs, it is quite likely that you will dream of being pregnant. As many people know, sometimes the changes we undergo do not feel altogether like a matter of choice. Sometimes it is as if the change chooses us. If you are considering a move, but have not made a conscious commitment or decision, your dreammaker may select a dream of pregnancy to symbolize the feeling of a natural force electing to move through you. There is a sense of inevitability about pregnancy and a sense that life will not be denied. You may deny your potential and growth just so long, and then, ready or not, you may find yourself taking actions that surprise and delight you.

Giving Birth

Dreams of giving birth have a similar association to the theme of pregnancy. Interestingly, men too sometimes dream of giving birth, since the symbolism has to do with bringing something new into the world. The implication is that the dreamer is responsible for the new item, and that there is often a kind of "labor" involved. As I worked upon my doctoral dissertation, I dreamed of giving birth to a book, and of pulling papers out of my womb. Think of the associations of childbirth. "Hard work, but worth it." (So my mother assures me.) "Often painful. Sometimes frightening." "Often transcendent, loving, miraculous." "New life emerging that is made of the same stuff you are." Buying a car, for example, would not generate a dream of giving birth, for the car would not be made of you, in that sense. Building a car, however, might cause you to have a childbirth dream, if the creation of the car was coming out of a deep place inside you.

Your Car

As I mentioned earlier, your car very often represents your identity. It can also symbolize travel—the way you get around. But more often than not your car is your professional self, or the predominant part of your conscious identity. Women who are pregnant will frequently dream of driving suddenly huge, unwieldy vehicles. So too will people who have taken on additional activities which seem gigantic to the subconscious mind. Getting a promotion may cause you to dream of driving a bus full of passengers (who are relying on your skills) and feeling anxious because you are unfamiliar with the controls. If you are considering whether to update your resume or to conduct a job search with the old one, you might dream of being passed by other drivers in more modern cars, while you putt along in an old gas-hog. This would, of course, be a tip from your dreammaker that you might be better off if you updated the resume. On the other hand, if you dreamed of people with pretentious, new-fangled cars breaking down along the highway, while you sailed smoothly along in your reliable Volvo, your dream would be telling you that your standard approach will get you where you want to go.

Lost Car

If you dream of misplacing your car keys or losing your car, it is likely that you are experiencing some confusion about your identity, and your ability to get where you want to go. An extremely talented friend of mine dreams often of parking his car and then of being unable to find it again. He often embarks on plans to enhance his professional image and then doubts his own judgement. Possibly because he can do so many things well, he is sometimes unsure of finding *his professional vehicle.* If you are embroiled in a situation that absorbs you and causes you to *lose yourself* in a way that holds you back, you may also dream of losing your car.

No Place to Park

A dream of wanting to stop your car yet being unable to find a suitable place to park will likely come about if you have sought and not found a suitable place for yourself. People who have settled in jobs they dislike but are unclear about what they *do* want, often have this dream. There is the sense that one has to do *something,* just as one has to park *somewhere,* whether a favorable place is found or not. A variation on this dream is trying to return to your car and finding that it is not in the pleasant place you where you thought you left it, but is in fact out on the street, or in a mud-puddle. This is often associated with disappointment about the current work or professional situation which looked good when you selected it, but which turned out differently than you expected.

Animals

Animals generally symbolize the characteristics they embody for the dreamer. If you dream about a goose, ask yourself what geese are like and how you feel about them. You may surprise yourself; and your feelings about the creature are all important. An attorney I know surprised me with his definition of a crocodile, saying they are considered vicious, but they are really just effective at what they do. He rather admired them, and felt that they were misjudged. Guess who the crocodile represented for him? The part of himself that was effective, considered dangerous, and was misjudged for his skill.

Domestic animals often, but not always, represent the cuddly, loving, naive aspect of the dreamer. If you dream of suddenly remembering that you have left your dog or cat out in the cold, or that you forgot to feed it, you are likely examining a part of yourself that you have forgotten to care for. It is common for people who are on the fast track in their careers to dream of forgetting to let their pet outside to play. This is fairly direct information from the subconscious about the very real need to give that aspect of the self some loving attention.

If you dream of a fish or mammal which fascinates you, but do not find a connection to your waking life at first glance, there is a possibility that the dreammaker is showing you a quality embodied in the animal which is an attribute you need to cultivate in your waking life. The power of a grizzly bear, the other-worldly wisdom of a whale, or the friskiness of a young colt may be available to you, but temporarily locked in the recesses of your deeper nature. Many native traditions believe that each of us has a "power animal" which offers unusual strengths uniquely suited to the individual. Martial art traditions similarly utilize the metaphor of animal techniques (such as the cat stance, or the cobra strike) as vehicles for understanding balance, courage, speed, and power. If you describe the animal and find no match in your waking life, "try on" this interpretation. How would it impact your current situation if you were to use the qualities inherent in the dream animal? If you were to use the patience and calm, unquestionable power of the elephant? The relaxed, but completely ready posture of the lion?

Loathsome Animals

It is common for unpleasant characteristics of loved ones or coworkers to be represented in dreams as frightening or disgusting animals. If you dream that you are sleeping with a rat, for example, take another look at your partner. What have you been afraid to see? Or, if you have no partner, are you "in bed with someone" in the business sense? Check your feelings about the animal, look for dream puns in its name, and look for any possibility of its representing a part of yourself of which you have been afraid or scornful.

Insects

Dreams of insects often refer to something that is "bugging" you. As always, take into account the entire dream action. If you dream of ants who work continually on a project that is then knocked down by passersby, you may be looking at your own inner experience of a futile project. The dream pun "in sex" sometimes appears when insects are involved and there are issues about hygiene or childhood programming against sexual expression.

Injury or Illness

Dream injuries are symbolic of current conditions. If you dream of losing your foot, you may be losing your footing, or feel unable to stand on your own two feet right now. Dreams of losing your voice may indicate a denial of your ability to speak up for yourself in waking life.

Take a look at the type of condition or injury, and its location within the body. What function does that part of the body serve? Does it allow you to take in air, to eliminate waste, or to support your own weight? (If you don't know, ask someone. For dream purposes, you can either obtain information from medical resources, or from persons who understand the symbolic function of the body parts such as a psychologists, therapists, or holistic health practitioners. I recommend books by Louise L. Hay, a marvelous writer and therapist, such as *You Can Heal Your Life,* and *Healing the Body,* for information about the symbolic meaning of certain maladies.) All images are not symbolic however. You may want to consider the literal implications of physical imagery.

It is possible for health information of which you had no conscious knowledge to appear in your dreams. I know of a woman who dreamed of a certain design and as part of her therapy her psychiatrist had her draw her dream images. When he saw her dream drawing he wasted no time in referring her to a physician. Without any understanding of what it was, she had drawn an enlargement of a cancer cell. She certainly had no conscious knowledge of what cancer cells look like. Upon examination it was discovered that she did have cancer. Fortunately, she was treated in time and eventually recovered. When dealing with the body, the dreammaker has a tremendous ability to detect changes, such as early pregnancy. Don't frighten yourself, because these dreams are often symbolic, but be practical about the information you receive. If you are inclined to a certain physical condition, and you dream of having it again, check it out. Remain aware of the symbolic implications of illness or injury. If you are going through trauma for whatever reason, you may well dream of dying, or of having some part of your body injured, even mutilated. This is generally a symbolic version of the pain you are going through in your waking life.

Interestingly, women sometimes dream of injuries, and especially of bleeding when approaching their menstrual period. Many women have noticed the timing of such dreams. For those who experience pain during that time, the dreams often involve scenarios of being wounded in a painful manner.

Age or Numbers

Numbers in a dream can be very helpful to your discovery of meaning, and they are always presented intentionally. If, in your dream a five-year-old child runs around, it is likely that the dream is about something that is five years old. It may be your college education, the job you have held for that time, the relationship you are in, or it may be about something that happened to you five years ago exactly.

If the action of your dream takes place on the second floor of a hotel, and you are currently in your second year at college, it is likely that this dream is addressing your education, and the temporary, "just visiting" quality that you experience on campus. Take whatever numbers appear in your dream, and use them as clues. If you keep trying, you will find that they have an often uncanny accuracy about your waking life.

Shopping

Shopping is usually a metaphor for choosing something, or surveying your options. The setting will be a clue for you. Are you at the discount rack? Is there some choice you are considering which you previously "discounted?" Are you in an exclusive, fabulous shop trying on haute couture? Is there some way you are about to splurge on a new vision of yourself? Are you buying clothes that are too expensive? Is your work self "costing too much" for the rest of your life? Are you in a huge mall with too many choices? Are you trying to find the "right choice" for this next stage of your life, but feeling overwhelmed by the myriad options and glossy packaging? If you are faced with the necessity of making a choice, but don't want to do any of the things you have contemplated, you may dream of going through a shopping area and *not seeing anything you like.* Use the shopping metaphor as a generalization and generate the description to pin down a personal meaning.

Going Home

Dreams about your childhood home frequently indicate that you are going through something that has a direct connection with your childhood. If you are dismayed to "awaken" in your childhood bed and feel trapped in an unhappy home again, you can be fairly sure you are feeling trapped in patterns from your childhood. On the other hand, if you recall disliking your childhood, and you dream of returning there and feeling that it isn't all that bad, you may need to consider that you have amplified some of those unhappy memories, making them more troublesome than the were the actual events.

If you dream of a current life situation, but the action takes place in your childhood home, you may consider whether you are looking at the situation from the perspective you had when you were a child living in that house. Are you reacting as if your boss is a powerful monster and you are a helpless kid? Are you re-living the loneliness, the left-out feeling you had as a child, inappropriately and unnecessarily now? Are you bringing your romantic partner home to live at the family house? This is a strong hint that your relational patterns are coming right out of childhood programming.

A High View

A dream in which you are looking at something from a high view is often an indication you are gaining a new perspective on something. You may be in a situation in which some people are lost, but your perspective allows you to see the "big picture." Times of breakthrough, such as deciding what direction to take, often bring on dreams of seeing things from a high vantage point.

Baby Clothes

Clothes that have been outgrown, or baby clothes, are often an indication that there is something that you have outgrown, which would be suitable to give away. Use the rest of the dream to pin-point your interpretation. If you find old, outgrown clothes at your place of work, you may be doing something you have outgrown. Similarly, if your clothes at home no longer "fit" you may have outgrown aspects of your personal life.

The Forgotten Baby

Forgotten baby dreams, like neglected pet dreams, are reflecting what I call "the abandoned self." The dream goes like this: You have a child, baby, or several children, which somehow you have forgotten you had. You have not been caring for them, feeding them, or tending them in any way. (You may even have given them away for adoption.) Realizing what you have done, you are stricken with remorse, even horror that you could have forgotten something so beloved. You may awaken feeling deeply troubled, with a sadness that haunts you throughout the day. Or you may awaken to find that you have been crying in your sleep.

Excluding situations in which the dream matches your literal past experience—these are dreams reminding you of aspects of yourself (or your life) that you have long overlooked, suppressed or "abandoned." The baby or child may represent a talent you have abandoned in favor of worldly concerns. Or it may be some part of you which is less dominant and therefore more vulnerable in the world. There is some part of you which needs support and care, without which it is fairly helpless. Often this much of a realization will permit recognition of what the baby represents. Describe the qualities of the baby or child. What is it like? What does it remind you of? How old is it? A fledgling project you abandoned will more likely be represented by a baby. Something you have not touched for five years will more likely be depicted by a five year old. Are there several children—several sides of yourself—that you have discarded? Does the dream recur often? If so, this is a signal that the timing is right to bring that part of your life in from the cold.

These dreams are delightfully precious and meaningful. However, they can also be disturbing and confusing. Many a newly divorced woman has confided in me that she now dreamed she was just starting to care for a baby that she hadn't realized she had. The image of sudden parenthood and divorce is not a pleasant one, yet when you realize such a dream is about finally having the freedom to nurture some part of the *self,* then the it begins to make perfect sense, and becomes a harbinger of growth rather than distress.

Dreams in the Bedroom

When the action of your dream takes place in the bedroom, this is a good indication that your sex life is at least a part of what is being reflected.

Dreams that begin in the bedroom and go elsewhere may show how your sexual issues travel with you throughout the day. When the reverse is true, and the action of the day winds up with you in the bedroom, you may be seeing how your work concerns are affecting the time you spend trying to be intimate.

If you are in a strange bedroom, describe the qualities of the room, how you feel there, and what you would expect to happen in such a room. Is it Victorian? (Old-fashioned, and restricted?) Is it lurid and bizarre with a large mirror on the ceiling? (Strange and a bit out of your league?) Is it the bedroom of your parents, or grandparents? (What did you learn from them about intimacy and sexuality? Are you attempting to live out a contemporary life with the definitions and expectations your grandparents or parents used?) Are you in the bed you had as a little boy or girl? (Are you trying to have a grown-up relationship, using the fantasy expectations of your childhood as a yard-stick of success?)

Someone Watching You Make Love

If someone is watching you make love in your dream, then you are likely examining how the opinions of others effect your intimate life. It is common to dream of your parents watching you, being in the room, or popping in while you are making love. Commonly those who watch have no reaction at all to your activities. You are embarrassed or concerned, but others simply speak to you or say hello, as if there were nothing out of the ordinary. In such cases, ask yourself if you are worrying unnecessarily about what others would think of your most private life.

Eating in a Cafeteria

In a cafeteria you slide your tray along all the offerings and take what you want. Dreams of eating in a cafeteria have to do with making choices. Do you refuse to make a selection because you don't see anything you like? Do you watch in disgust as fellow diners select things that you wouldn't dream of "eating?" If you do pick something, how do you like it? Is it expensive? Is it something you loved as a child? The further meanings of your associations to your selection can give you valuable information about the waking choices you are facing.

Looking at a Menu

Looking at a menu is also about making a choice. You are surveying what is available, using the description to determine what it will probably be like when it comes to you, and gauging the cost to you as well. Pay attention to what you select, your reasons for doing so, and what your reactions are to the meal that you select. If you have just taken on a new position or project and that night dream of being served something that is not at all what you wanted, you may be on the lookout for a few curves ahead in the project.

Eating, Doing, or Buying Something too Costly

These dreams contain insight about some part of your life, a habit, practice, or activity that is costing you dearly. My dream of eating a dessert that cost $19.00 is an example. In that case, the symbolism of a dessert and sweets was fairly literal. Look at what you are buying (or deciding not to buy) to get a clue to the part of life you are viewing. Is it something having to do with work? Your appearance? Making a good impression? Doing something you no longer believe in, but feel trapped into continuing? Many times the dreamer will say, "I'm not paying that," or, "I'll never do that again." Such dreams are attempting to illustrate the exorbitant cost of a behavior or situation to the dreamer's well-being. These episodes can be amusing, but their message should be taken seriously.

Dreams of Famous People

While it can be fun to spend the evening with a famous person, there are usually two explanations for these dreams. The first is that the famous person is reflecting either a person of similar qualities in your waking life, or an aspect of your own personality that has resonant qualities. Describe the qualities of the celebrity and ask, "Is there anyone in my life, or any part of myself that this reminds me of?" The first thing that pops into your mind is usually the correct association.

When the similarities are to an aspect of yourself, don't be embarrassed to say so. If the famous person is someone you greatly admire this can get a bit tricky. The most common reaction from my students is that there *are* some similarities, but the famous person is much more wonderful. Remember that dreams tend to exaggerate and amplify in order to communicate. Your celebrity may in fact be an exaggeration of some facet of yourself, but don't deny these qualities in yourself. The presence of the celebrity may be a clue that you need to give yourself permission to recognize these qualities in yourself and to "celebrate" them.

The second purpose of these dreams is to suggest the addition of a certain element to your present situation. If you dream of Cher coming in and telling off your boss in her no nonsense way, you might want to consider a more direct approach. Or if you dream that Perry Mason comes in and defends you, you might think about speaking up in your own defense more often. Try these approaches on mentally and see if they seem sound. Don't rush out and do something horrendous, but consider the addition of certain styles, certain ways of operating in your current situation. It may be that like adding spice to a favorite recipe, you will find adding something unusual is just what your situation needed.

Old Friends

If an old friend whom you no longer see in waking life appears in your dream, it is highly likely that he or she is representing a quality you associate with that person. Ask yourself a few questions: If you could describe this friend in one or two words, what would you say? Allow yourself to speak in generalities and themes. Don't concern yourself with being "politically correct." Stereotypes are fine in this instance. For example, you might dream about a young woman you knew as a teenager, who was considered the "school slut." Or you may dream about a friend who always made you feel inferior, just by virtue of his popularity and good fortune. You might think of him as a "top dog." Once you have identified the quality of this person, you can then proceed to check who or what in your current situation has a similar quality. Did someone make you feel inferior recently, or did you do it yourself by making inappropriate comparisons? One woman accidently said yes to setting dates with two different men for the same night. She was so appalled by her oversight that her dreammaker used her high school's "bad girl" in her dream that night.

Sometimes you will be unable to find a qualitative "handle" for the old friend. In those cases, describe the quality of your life when you were associated with that person. Were those the "good old days?" Were those the days when you "went along with the crowd?" Were those times when you first began feeling you were a sexual being? Whatever the theme was during that time of your life may be symbolized by the old friend making a reappearance. In such cases, the old friend is like a trigger for a memory rather like the first few bars of a familiar song. Just being with them in the dream brings back all that went with that time in your past. The purpose of such an appearance is generally one of two things: First, there is something going on in your life that is similar to what went on during that time in the past. Check for the emotional undertones. The second possibility is that you are craving a certain quality that was present in your life at that time. Dreams *do* bring to us experiences that we need in order to feel balanced. If you have no playful, boisterous friends presently, you may get to have that kind of relationship in your dream again. And it will nourish your spirit, just it would if you experienced it in waking life.

Police

Dreams of police sometimes have to do with how you relate to authority in your life. Police represent those people who are supposed to protect us, yet who most often announce that we are "in trouble." If you dream of being hassled by the police, you may be worried about getting an income tax audit, or about your father coming to visit you, or some other element in your life that has to do with an authority figure.

Car Breaking Down

In dreams depicting your car breaking down, getting in an accident, or needing to be taken in for repair, the symbolism may actually reflect your physical condition. One woman who described a dream of taking her car in for the repair of a broken axle was later told by her chiropractor that her hips and pelvis were slightly misaligned. A man involved in physical labor too strenuous for him dreamed of a twisted bumper buckling and hanging awkwardly from his car. Pay particular attention to the part of the car that gets damaged or breaks down, and check to see if there is an analogous part of yourself that is in need of attention.

Death of a Loved One

There is nothing so frightening as the possibility of losing a child or a loved one. Dreams that depict the death of a loved one are among the most disturbing and memorable dreams of all. Even years after such a dream, individuals who came to me for other reasons will take the time to inquire about death imagery.

It is important to note that in every case of this kind, the person who "died" in the dream was still healthy and thriving years later. When examining these dreams, you will want to recall the three levels of meaning your dream may contain:
1. Literal
2. Symbolic/Psychological
3. Psycho-Spiritual

If your loved one is in no danger that you can see, but is in fact preparing to go off to college for the first time, you may assume the dream is dealing with the "death" of an era or life passage. It is not uncommon for the mother of a bride to dream of her daughter's death shortly before the wedding. This appears to be less a commentary upon matrimony than a private opportunity to say good-bye to and mourn the person that the daughter *will never be again*. Ask yourself what changes are occurring in your life that could be felt as a kind of loss or a "mini-death," and you will be likely to discover that these "deaths" are also symbolic of new beginnings.

Chapter 7

Keys to Understanding Symbols

It may take time for you to get accustomed to thinking metaphorically about your dreams. If you are good at analyzing problems logically in waking life, the shift to symbolism may be tricky for you. But the good news is that once you get the hang of working with the symbolism in dreams, you're going to have a field day because your powers of logic and ability to recognize patterns will be powerful assets. There really is a kind of logic to dreams, and certain rules that tend to hold true, just as in math or any discipline. If you work with your dreams consistently, you'll discover some of the rules of symbolism too. To give you a head start, here are some of the tendencies I've observed in the way dreams use symbols. As you read, keep in mind that there are general rules that are true more often than not. They will give you a short cut with many dreams, but always decide for yourself whether or not they apply to the particular dream you're working with.

Weather Conditions and Climate

Although the weather conditions in your dream are usually part of the background; they can reveal important things about what you're going through. Weather can be thought of as the emotional barometer of the dreamer's experience and the feelings involved in your situation.

Stormy Weather

For example stormy weather often reflects tempestuous feelings or recent arguments, particularly in the home. People seldom report stormy conditions in dreams dealing with work issues. Tornadoes, floods and blizzards usually are clues that you're dreaming about family matters or relationship issues. Just as real life storms arise from different forces coming together, so storms in dreams tend to reflect conflict of some kind. The conflict or mixed forces are most often between the dreamer and her loved ones, or between different sides of herself. Stormy dreams are not always signs of trouble, but they can provide greater awareness that something is stirring up some deep feelings in you. Stormy dreams signal times when we can be thrown off balance because of inner turmoil or the chaos around us. This may be a time to seek out stability by consulting trusted friends and the steadying influences in your life, and you may want to be cautious about over-reacting and making snap decisions.

Snowfall

When you have a dream of wandering through a snow covered landscape, or being in falling snow it is probable that you're going through an ending of some kind. Winter landscapes arise in dreams most often when there has been a loss, a break-up, or the closing of some chapter in our lives. This is most likely to be the case if you dream of a winter scene during another season. But winter scenes do more than reflect the end of something, and our sadness about that. Implied in the image of winter is a certain trust in nature. Though the image conveys the end or "death" of something, it also suggests that in a larger sense this is merely a season in your life. If you can trust, endure and care for yourself through this time, you will be rewarded by the inevitable emergence of spring, and the new options and hope it implies.

Rain

Rain is often associated with sadness, as if your entire dream were shedding tears. The intensity of rainfall in your dream can serve to show that you may be "saturated" with sadness or emotion just now. Pouring rain often happens in dreams when you are going through divorce or an unwanted change that is deeply saddening. If this fits your situation, you can support yourself by realizing this is a kind of grieving process, and that you may feel swept along for awhile. Rain like this does not indicate a mistake. It merely tends to act out feelings that may have no appropriate outlet by day.

Fog

A surprisingly common element in dreams is that of having to navigate or drive through heavy fog. This difficult task reflects a current challenge that has the following characteristics. It is difficult to know what is right, hard to keep your bearings, and impossible to know where you are in relation to your goals and potential hazards. In other words, something in this situation throws you off so that you aren't as sure of yourself as you normally are. Not only are the rules of this game confusing, but they stir up your personal cloudbank of old issues and mess with your powers of judgement. If this seems on target for your situation, then abide by the rules for driving through fog. Slow down. Proceed with caution. Keep switching your perspective by looking immediately ahead of you and then trying to see into the distance as well. Don't assume that the others involved know what they're doing right now, because they probably are engulfed in fog (confusion) too. The positive note about this image is that, like real fog, it reflects a situation that takes over completely for a while, but is by its very nature, inherently a temporary condition. Even if the challenge is enduring, your confusion about it will not last.

Darkness

Have you ever noticed how many of your dreams are set at night or in darkness? When the action of your dream takes place at night, the implication is that you are dealing with a situation that is confusing or difficult to understand. This can happen when the pros and cons of a problem are obvious but your feelings are mixed up or don't make sense. Darkness isn't a symbol of evil as many people think, nor a sign that you are struggling with "dark forces" in your psyche. Instead,

I believe darkness shows that you are traveling in unmarked territory in this current situation. You may be striving toward a goal, but mystified that you always seem to make choices that sabotage your efforts. Or, you may be doing all you can to attract a mate, but finding yourself moving through a series of disastrous liaisons instead. Darkness implies that the basic nature of what you're dealing with right now is elusive to you on a conscious level, and that when you do understand it, it may not seem logical or sensible to you at all. If this makes sense, give yourself permission to be "in the dark" about your present circumstances for awhile. Don't expect that everything will make sense in a neat and tidy way, or that your official stance on the situation reflects your whole spectrum of feelings and needs. The more tolerant your are of mixed feelings and subtle influences in yourself, the sooner everything will begin to fall into place for you.

Sunshine

Sunshine and bright pleasant weather is usually a sign of positive feelings and a time of optimism. You may dream of a glowing day when you have turned the corner with a problem that had plagued you, or when something positive is happening in your life. Dawn is usually a symbol of the start of a new chapter in your life, and it's typical to have a surprising "new day" setting for a dream after you have emerged from a trying or confusing time. You may still have other dreams that reflect the challenges in your situation, but if you've had such a "sunny" dream, it is safe to say that you're entering the beginning of something that will ultimately be positive.

Desert

Dreams set in the desert usually take place when some part of your life feels barren or stark. If you've transferred to a new city and have no friends yet, or are somehow estranged from the people and activities that are familiar to you, the scene of wandering the desert suggests you feel separated from everything that nourishes you. If you're dealing with a sudden change or disruption in your life, you can use common sense to reach out to others and to pursue activities that you love. If you believe the dream desert is reflecting a more enduring kind deprivation, then you'll have to consider carefully what you can do to make life more lush and fertile again.

Jungle/Tropics

Tropical settings are common in dreams, particularly jungles. This background reflects two primary qualities: rich potentials, and hidden hazards. Jungle dreams most often pertain to career issues and the pressure to cash in on opportunities without falling prey to competitors, critics or "traps." If your dream is set in a jungle motif you can assume you are dealing with something that stirs your sense of adventure and pushes you a bit. Tropical paradises on the other hand are far less common in dreams, but they usually reflect a situation rich with potential benefit and enjoyment. Just as jungles tend to deal with career questions, tropical paradise dreams are more typically focused on relationship and personal arenas.

Size and Proximity

You may have noticed that dreams place you in strange predicaments, such as reeling a killer whale into your rubber raft, or waking up with a giant spider on your face. In addition to the symbolic meaning of any given object or creature, it's size and proximity to you are also very telling.

Large Size

When something is unusually large in proportion to you in a dream, this can mean that the item or creature represents something that is "a big deal" to you. Because dreams are more concerned with your inner experience, the giant monster may not be something that others would consider that important, but it is something that looms large in your experience. Large size can also reflect something that bothered you as a youngster. If your first go-round with a scary neighbor or a nasty bully took place when you were quite small, then your mind may imprint the horror of having someone large push you down, control or intimidate you. Later in life, when a similar pressure or fear triggers anxiety, you might then dream of an oversized creature chasing you, or a truck or building that seemed about to fall on you and trap you. Finally, there are many times in dreams when a tiny thing, such as an insect or a small animal, is enlarged so that it becomes monstrous. When this happens, it can indicate that a situation that is objectively minor is having a powerful effect on you. You may be magnifying the situation yourself, or it may be that your history or sensitivity makes it very difficult to tolerate. Whatever the cause of the magnification is, be cautious with the way you handle others, and compassionate toward your own needs and reactions.

Closeness and Distance

When something in a dream is right on top of you, in your face, or down your neck, you can bet it represents something that is prominent in your present circumstances. If the object or creature in question is on you or has invaded your clothes, then the factor in question also has an invasive quality as disruptive as it is disquieting. Things that are in the distance usually represent factors that you wish to move toward or away from in the future. This doesn't mean these factors are your "destiny" but it does mean they are things you can see on the horizon and may have strong feelings about.

Things above You

Most often things above us in dreams represent the future or factors we aspire to. Climbing mountains, ladders, hills and obstacle courses can reflect arduous progress toward a desired goal or destination. The general rule is that if you are moving toward the high place, then you are dreaming about progress toward a goal. If you are not moving but are witnessing something above you, or coming toward you in the sky, then you may be dreaming of something that seems to be looming in your future. (Again, this is not necessarily a concrete future or fate, it is the future assumed by your mind at the time of the dream.)

Downward Slant

If you are moving downhill in a dream, you may be either coasting in an easier mode than normal or feeling that you are losing ground with something you care about. If the downhill slide is frightening or feels like you have no control over it, it likely represents a situation that is proving resistant to your best efforts. If this is true for you, it may be time to reexamine your strategy for solving a certain problem, particularly if logic and favorite methods are not effective this time.

Space and Constriction

Just as weather can reflect your inner emotional climate, and height and size can reveal importance; the amount of space you have in your dream can also be significant. It is very uncomfortable to have too little room, and its unnerving in a dream to step off into oblivion or an endless void. The amount of space in your dream setting reflects the way you feel in your current situation. Are you cramped? Lost in space?

Too Much Space

It's been my experience that the majority of people who report unnerving dreams of too much space are men. Typically their spacious nightmares involve stepping into a void or off the edge into a bottomless pit. Although Freud might make some swift inferences about sexuality regarding these dreams, I suspect there is more to them than fear of women's genitalia, or fear of the womb. Space is frightening because it is un-known, disorienting and provides no guidelines or clues about where we are. Any situation that strips away the familiar and casts us into the void can catalyze such a dream. A reason-able response to this dream would seem to be supporting your safari into the unknown, acknowledging that you may not be comfortable for a while as you pass through this phase, and reconnecting with intangible (but more permanent) factors in your life that cannot be lost.

Being Cramped

Typically, women report more dreams of being in rooms (as well as clothes and shoes) that are much too small for them. They slouch to make themselves smaller, crouch to fit into their tiny rooms or homes, and make themselves progressively smaller to try and fit through an hallway that grows ever more narrow. The lack of space in such dreams suggests a lack of choices or mental room to be yourself. It also may reflect a coping strategy of making yourself "fit" situations that don't really fit you. When this is true, then it is worth remembering that the adaptive strategy that makes poor circumstances tolerable is meant to be a temporary adjustment, not a permanent distortion of self.

Summary

Don't feel you must obsess about every item or nuance of a dream. You will be able to discover whatever you want to know by moving through the 5 steps and paying attention to what stands out to you. Just be aware that every element of your dream is included with a kind of purposeful intelligence. Just as the punctuation of a sentence makes it possible to understand it's rhythm and expression, so the setting and background of your dream are all intended to communicate the elements of your situation and feelings.

Chapter 8

Extraordinary Dreams

Some dreams need to be considered with special attention because something very unusual about them places them in a category of their own. **Recurring dreams, theme dreams, and dreams of spiritual guidance,** are examples of those that should be attended to and examined with diligence.

Recurring dreams need to be examined carefully because the dreamer is being given the same message repeatedly. Often recurring dreams will escalate in intensity until the dreamer "gets" the message, or makes some kind of change in the waking situation. As in the case of my recurring nightmares of being murdered, they stopped immediately after I left the job I found so "deadly."

Some people will have a recurring dream off-and-on for years. In these cases the dream is usually addressing a theme which the person continues to encounter in waking life. The dream is coming to you now because of something that is going on in your life *now*. Often the dreamer will be so accustomed to a dream that she will think, "Oh, this is that bottomless-pit dream again." Growing accustomed to something may actually blind you to its significance. Recurring dreams are signals to *pay attention*, not merely remnants from the past.

The basic approach to understanding such a dream is the same as described earlier: look at action metaphors, exaggerated feelings, and symbols. Describe these, and link the description to waking events. The dreamer needs to be aware of the cyclical nature of the pattern of these dreams. Something is happening in current life that has happened many times before, or at least the *psychological nature* of what is happening is the same as it has been in times past.

For example, if you dream of your parents scolding you or disciplining you long into adulthood, you may still be sorting out your desire to please versus your desire for independence.

Take the time to understand recurring dreams, because they are being repeated deliberately, and their meaning tends to be very important. These dreams are not, however, something to be feared. Recurring dreams are a kind of psychic balancing act that is being performed on your behalf. They are always working in your favor, and should be regarded as a source of valuable insight. People who have had recurring dreams for years may react to them with dread, especially if they are unpleasant or frightening. Generally speaking, the meaning you uncover will not be nearly as frightening as the dreams themselves.

Recurring dreams are also linked with certain life passages. Children may have the same dream until they reach puberty, or until they graduate from high school and leave the parental home. Then the dreams may disappear. Some may have certain dreams repeatedly during college years which will stop upon graduation. Still other recurring dreams will be associated with early marriage and childbearing years for women. The start of a "new life" passage, such as after a divorce or during the launching of a new business, can signal the beginning of a recurring dream associated with that period.

Don't be afraid that recurring dreams indicate there is something wrong with you. They usually indicate what is wrong with your *situation* instead.

While some recurring dreams *do* stem from traumatic events, such as childhood molestation or combat experience, recurring dreams should not be assumed to be signals of "emotional scars," or "shocking secrets." The dreamer will usually have conscious awareness of association to a trauma, if one is problematic; yet the real value of the recurring dream is not in uncovering the past per se, but rather in illustrating the way(s) in which the past may be impacting the present.

In cases where the recurring dream is lurid, sexual, or violent in nature, you may be relieved of concern by working to understand it. (Get assistance, or keep researching until you are satisfied.) In most cases, the shocking, even sickening quality of the dream is not an indication of pathology or "something wrong" with the dreamer, but is an attempt to convey information long overlooked by presenting it repeatedly in a manner which cannot comfortably be ignored.

You may need to give yourself formal permission to explore feeling and be analytical at the same time. Many of us attempt to live with the illusion that we can either be swept away by feelings, or we can act, but never both. Recurring dreams that elude comprehension are usually an indication of a strong split between reasoning and feeling. Dreamwork is one arena in which you must allow the presence of strong feelings to "be there" even while you dissect dream imagery with meticulous care. Assume you can do this, that it will not hurt you, and that you will successfully uncover the meaning you seek.

Theme dreams are similar to recurring dreams, except that they are rather like similar episodes from different television programs; the plot and action are the same, but the characters and setting may change. The dreammaker is attempting to make you aware of a situation by letting you look at it in different ways. When theme dreams occur intermittently during your lifetime, they are often an indication that you are experiencing *similar types of challenges* in different situations. You may have a typical style of reacting to situations which your dreammaker is attempting to show you. For example to dream repeatedly of someone insulting you slightly, and of pulling out a sword and executing them, may show that you tend to overreact to criticism by "cutting someone off" completely.

It is not unusual to develop theme dreams during certain life passages. As with recurring dreams, these will tend to stop when the life passage is over. If such a dream returns after years have gone by, you will begin to better understand its meaning by looking at the passage of life *during which the dream first began.* Here is a dream I had frequently as a child:

> *I am trying to tunnel out of a military prison camp. I have dug out an excellent underground tunnel, and am ready to make my escape. I believe that if I am caught I may be killed, but I can't stand the confinement any longer. I decide to take as many people with me as I possibly can.*

When I was old enough to move out of my parents home and attend college the dreams of prison camp stopped. Although our home was not an abusive one, and it was pleasant in many ways, a strict code of behavior prevailed which my rather creative spirit found very confining. In later years, whenever I would distort myself to accommodate the expectations of others, either at work or in relationships, I would again dream of tunneling out of prison. Examining these dreams, and the times at which they appeared in my life has helped me to recognize how vital a part of my well-being is sacrificed when I try to "confine" my more genuine self.

As with recurring dreams the survivor of a traumatic event may have nightmares about the event off-and-on throughout life. Again, it is worthwhile to note that the theme dreams are in relationship to something that is occurring in the waking life. It is also important to acknowledge that incidents which were not objectively horrifying can be just as devastating in subjective experience.

For many of us, our earliest doubts about our self-worth were in a sense emotionally imprinted. If the circumstances surrounding those early feelings were sexual, then the subconscious may tend to adopt sexual imagery in dreams to depict *any* feelings of violation or personal compromise. If the circumstances were violent, or paralyzing, then the subconscious may compose dreams using images of physical battle or premature burial.

One woman complained to me that decades after leaving an addictive relationship with an abusive husband, she still was haunted periodically by dreams of him. She asked me frankly if this meant she was still "hooked" on him after all these years. I explained that was only *one* possibility. Instead, we looked at her personal style during that relationship. What had life been like for her then? She confided that she had been riddled with self-doubt, insecurity, and had been too ready to compromise for the sake of bolstering the relationship. "Co-dependent stuff," she said. I asked her to consider whether the symbol of her ex-husband was dream shorthand for an entire constellation of actions and compromises she engaged in during that marriage. Her ex-husband would appear in her dreams when she was behaving similarly in current situations. She would have these dreams when she was reverting to self-negating behaviors. She agreed that this felt quite accurate. She valued learning this "signal" from her dreammaker, and was relieved to learn she wasn't carrying a torch for her ex-husband.

Sometimes theme dreams will depict a subjective experience of a situation which you feel forced to deny in waking hours. Here is the dream of Ellen, a fellow graduate student in psychology, who found our initial training in therapy to be emotionally challenging. She had many dreams of this nature, at least once a week, after beginning her training to become a therapist.

> I am swimming in waters that are filthy. There is a heavy coating of sludge on the water. At some places the water is completely solid, and I have to get out and walk on the stinking crusts that have formed. I hate to get back in that water. I look down at myself and see that I am filthy. I have so far to go. It stretches out in front of me, and I have such a long way to go to get to the land. I don't want to be doing this, but it's too late, I'm in the middle of it. It all seems very familiar to me.

Ellen had this dream frequently during her first year of training. After that, however, she began to dream of swimming in waters that were clear and pleasant. Sometimes she swam well, at other times she was afraid of the waters, but the environment was no longer polluted and rancid. Ellen had been suffering, as so many of us in psychology do, from a tendency to self-diagnose and find fault with her every thought and feeling. She had trouble with the strong emotions that came up during her training, and then blamed herself for her lack of expertise. The result was that she decided she had "everything in the book" wrong with her. *She saw that she was filthy.* In addition to her self-critical style, emotions that had been long "crusted-over" were beginning to come lose through her studies. Committed to a long course of study to become a psychologist, she regretted her choice during that first arduous year, but was already "in the middle of it." The sense of familiarity she experienced is quite common in theme dreams. Since these themes *are* ongoing parts of our waking experience, they will often give the dreamer a sense of having done this before or will cause you to think "this is something I do all the time."

Dreams of Spiritual Guidance

Over the past decade I have come to appreciate that dreams encompass realms of what appear to be spiritual content. This is hardly surprising, since philosophical and spiritual questions are a part of life. During my early training, I was leery of slapping transpersonal or esoteric interpretations on dreams which I suspected were more related to everyday information. However, my own experience, as well as my work with others has led me to make the following recommendation.

Trust yourself, trust your experience, and keep your mind open to explore even the unknown.

Our present understandings about the capacity of the human mind and spirit are currently undergoing considerable alteration. Experiences of paranormal and psychic phenomena are becoming so common that most people have an intuitive understanding that such things are quite real, even though our scientific paradigms must expand in order to explain the mechanisms involved. The working style I use in examining dreams which may have spiritual implications is this: Look at literal meaning first. If literal meaning would be silly or inappropriate, then consider the symbolic level of interpretation as we have been discussing. If that level of understanding seems inadequate (and here you must rely on your subjective *feeling*), then be open to the possibility of spiritual information. Native peoples have long accepted the use of dreams as vehicles for communicating between dimensions or planes of reality. The Bible is full of references to people receiving guidance and information about their faith "in dreams."

The reflection of life contained in dreams holds more information than we recognize in our conscious awareness. It is entirely possible that spiritual understandings are also revealed within that reflection. A balance of common-sense and open-mindedness is most practical, and will lead you to the most accurate interpretation.

Verbal Transmittals

Occasionally I encounter someone who has a strange and fascinating type of dream which I call a *verbal transmittal.* These dreams contain no plot, often no visual aspect at all, no characters and no action. (Possibly in later years we will discover that these are not dreams at all, but at this point, I treat them as such and consider their input extremely valuable.) The dreamer will be asleep, but "conscious" in a sense, and will simply hear a disembodied voice telling them something. This may sound quite spooky, but with the naturalness of all dreams this is just the way it happens.

Typically the message will be brief and will be of practical value to the dreamer. Dietary suggestions, directions to take safety precautions, or comments about spiritual practices may occur. The voice is usually clear and speaks in a matter-of-fact way. Dreamers are often told to quit smoking, to get more rest or to stick with a challenging course of action. Naturally you would not want to follow the suggestions of these transmittals if they struck you as being unhealthy in some way. However, in all the transmittals I have examined, I have never encountered a suggestion that was not wholesome and beneficial. Some people awaken with the awareness that someone has been talking to them, explaining something, but they will have no recollection of the content.

Since my earliest memory I have had "transmittal" dreams, which have the quality of tuning into an educational broadcast during sleep. Explanations or lectures will be given, sometimes for what seem to be hours, on diverse topics at rapid speed. I am aware of nothing except the voice and the words, and the topics are not necessarily those about which I have any conscious interest.

I encounter a number of people who have similar experiences, and I would be interested in hearing from you if you recall such dreams. (My mailing address is in the back of the book.) There are those who believe that these "transmittal" dreams are a matter of psychic eavesdropping, that perhaps the mind's "extra-sensory perception" is no longer blocked by conscious thought and thus we "hear" information from different sources during sleep. Still others believe such dreams to be examples of channeling: receiving information from paranormal sources, such as spirit guides. These dreams do seem to occur more frequently among children, older people, and those who make a practice of meditation. It may be that, as with all dreams, many people have them and simply fail to recall them. I believe these occurrences *are* non-ordinary in some way, although their origin is still unclear. When dealing with the unknown, history indicates that those who keep an open inquisitive mind gain more from new developments than do those who pour energy into denying any experience that challenges the boundaries of their beliefs.

Spiritual Dreams and Visions

One reason I have been hesitant to write and speak about spiritual dreams is because I have seen so many people being passive, even masochistic, in the name of their spiritual beliefs. There is a powerful temptation in humans to try to explain one's suffering in ways that make it more meaningful without doing anything to change it. Beliefs about Karma, or past lives, can easily be turned into reasons to remain with dangerous or unacceptable conditions.

The greatest value dreams hold may be in the possibilities they present for *moving on*, for growing internally and releasing externally what you have outgrown. A preoccupation with the past, whether metaphysically or psychologically oriented, may obscure your view of the present. The question to ask then, in considering the spiritual elements in dreams, is how the information *enables* you, and increases your choices in life.

In recent years I have recognized within my own dreams, as well as those of my students, the struggle to integrate spiritual understandings with waking life experiences. Dreams are a natural avenue through which to experience the profundity of our understandings. They also are marvelous lie-detectors which prevent us from being out-of-touch when we need to take action immediately and process later. Some dream analysts don't wish to acknowledge the possibility that past-life excerpts can be revealed in dreams. Still others are exclusively interested in the New Age movement and tend to view all dreams from a psychospiritual vantage point which may ultimately be accurate, but which is elaborate and confusing to work with. In order to obtain the greatest benefit from your dream messages, it is critical to recall that they pertain to your current life situation. If what you consider to be a past life scene does come up in a dream, it is being presented to you because it is pertinent to your current situation. Whether the dreammaker is using a costume saga as a metaphor or you are viewing something that actually happened is up to you to decide. Too great an attachment to one point of view can inhibit your ability to understand your dreams. Be willing to see what is there, and don't get side-tracked from your intention to understand what your dream has to offer you.

Some dreams can be so wonderful that you miss their sense of magic when you awaken.

Sometimes our dreams can be so magical that we long for that sense of transcendence during our waking hours as well. Many people dream of having a guide or teacher take them to a vantage point and show them something significant they need to know. Still others have been taken to places designed for education during dreams and attended entire lectures.

These experiences do appear to be of a different nature than ordinary dreams. I recommend you begin to attend to the sense of how "real" your dreams seem to you. Some feel quite floaty, misty, or otherwise consistent with the quality of dreams. Others are intriguing because the dreamer feels that they actually *are* performing "impossible" actions, or *are* speaking with angels or aliens. The value of these dreams may be three-fold. First, they contain information that is pertinent to current life situations. Second, they challenge our understanding of what is possible—and the assumption that waking events are "real" and dream events are "imaginary." Third, they impact the personality, mind, and feelings of the dreamer as if they were "real." Thus growth, change, and personal evolution *are* accomplished through these events of the night. They are after all experiences that you have lived through, and they become a part of your history. If you have such dreams I urge you to keep a record of what you learn, as well as a careful record of their frequency and correspondence with your waking life situation.

Light Treatments

In recent years I have noticed an interesting type of dream emerging in my students' reports. It is possible that people are becoming more comfortable in discussing unusual dreams, or that these are dreams which tend to develop among people who meditate or follow a practice which fosters psychic development. It is also possible that as I have become more open-minded, I am recognizing certain types of experiences without rationalizing them away. I call these dreams *Light Treatments* because the only action they contain is that the dreamer is exposed to a very intense light. Here is a light treatment dream recently told to me.

I am lying in bed and I see a great deal of light across the room from me. I think that I have left the shutters open, and that light is seeping in. I open my eyes and am surprised to find that it is still dark out. I close my eyes, and almost immediately begin seeing the light again. It moves across the room to me. It is a big ball of light in front of me for a moment, and then it goes into my forehead and all through me. It dissipates. Then soon, there is another light across the room and it all repeats again. This goes on for quite a while. I have the sense that this is nourishing or charging me in some way. I like it. And then I just fall asleep.

This dreamer had been following a spiritual practice for many years of meditation, prayer, and a wholesome life-style. She was, in fact, quite conservative in her life-style, and somewhat skeptical of fringe groups and unorthodox concepts. I was pleased to learn of her experience, because if she said it happened this way, I have virtually no doubt that it did. She has since told me this dream comes to her once or twice a week. This woman awakens in the morning with a nice sense of having been rejuvenated during the night.

During a particularly sad period of my life I was searching for a professional direction of some sort and moved to a new city and state to investigate educational possibilities. I felt lonely and peculiar; unlike myself in a sense, and I missed the young man I had been seeing before the move. I experienced the following light treatment dream:

I am being taken by these light people to a great lake made of light. They are taking care of me because I have been so depressed lately. They carry me to the lake and dip me in the waters of light. I absorb some of the light each time they do so. Eventually I am radiant, almost as bright as the beings who are caring for me.

I awakened from this dream so moved by the caring of the light people that I felt renewed by the loving experience. I looked at myself in the mirror and although I didn't appear particularly radiant, neither did I appear as sad as I had the night before. I *did* feel I had undergone some kind of healing treatment, and was able to proceed with my educational plans with renewed vigor. Were these light people aiding me in lifting my vibration out of despair and loneliness? I tend to believe in the possibility. Historically, light emanations have long been associated with spiritually uplifting events. If you dream of intense light that feels loving, protective or nourishing, it is possible that you are receiving a kind of direct, almost electrical nourishment which is spiritual in nature.

Years prior to my move to attend graduate school I had a series of light treatment dreams which continued for a period of about six months.

> *I am held up to the light by several light people. They carry me upwards higher and higher into the light until I can't stand the intensity. Then I tell them I can't handle it and they just hold me at that level. It is a kind of light that shines right through me, which I absorb somehow. I can only absorb so much. I have the idea that this is occurring to change me in some way, but not to harm me, and this is not like a near death experience. The light is not in a tunnel, but is all over, in and through everything.*

I intuitively felt that in these dreams I was somehow being nourished and strengthened. I had the subjective experience that these were *events* rather than dream images, and I even experienced some fatigue at not being left alone to sleep some nights. Because these were pleasant, non-threatening experiences which seemed to strengthen my intuitive abilities and sense of direction, I was unconcerned by them. They were interesting, but during the day I tended to forget about these forays into the light spectrum, and only recalled the nightly field trips as they commenced each evening. Subsequently I have heard others' dreams of light treatments and I am curious about their origin and effects. Are they events rather than dreams? Are they indeed some kind of natural healing phenomenon that occurs during sleep? Could such dreams be brought on intentionally, lucidly, and used for purposeful self-renewal and healing? One interesting facet of these dreams is the experience of undergoing a *treatment* of some kind, rather than moving through the actions and feelings of a dream. If the nature of these dream events is in fact healing, then further investigations of them may hold potential benefits.

Spiritual Guides

In recent years I have heard more and more dreams in which an apparently wise being appears and provides direction to the dreamer. Some of these appearances provide the dreamer with a kind of question-and-answer period in which to learn from the teacher. Many times there is no visual aspect or plot to these dreams. They may consist entirely of a voice answering the dreamer's questions. Understanding the content of such dreams is easy because it is offered in direct language. The challenge is in considering what these dreams *are*. Are they indeed spiritual coaching sessions? Many would say yes. My recommendation would be to accept your own experience of them.

For some, the sensation of conversing with another intelligent being is so palpable there is no question that the experience was in any way illusory. Others assume all experiences occurring during sleep are dreams and are therefore "not real." Since I spend a great deal of time examining the realm of dreams, I tend to believe that dreams *are* real but in a different way than events of waking reality. I urge you to honor your experiences and the events you have lived through. If you dreamed it, you lived through it, internally at least.

When considering the advice given in these conversations, use common sense. If your visiting coach tells you to get more exercise, and you know that you need to do so, then you can feel fine about taking some steps in that direction. If you are told to run exactly 19 miles the next day, and you are not a runner at all, then you want to take that advise with a grain of salt. I have never heard of someone being given idiotic or harmful advice in these dreams, but *always* run information through your own filter of discernment before following it.

Dreams of the deceased

Many of us have dreams about people who are deceased. In general, most people believe that these are dreams in which the dreamer is given the opportunity to sort through the layers of emotion surrounding the lost loved one. When deciphering such dreams, you may want to assume that the loved one is being used by the dreammaker to exemplify a quality or to communicate something that you would not be able to "hear" from someone else. It is common to dream of the departed upon the anniversary of their passing, or upon another important anniversary you had together. If you frequently dream of someone no longer here, who was not particularly close to you, nor important in your life, then you may assume that character is representing something symbolically. Use the technique of describing the character to yourself, and then checking what that description reminds you of. It may well be an aspect of yourself that you refuse to develop or "give a voice to" in your waking reality. *That* is why the dreammaker is using an actor who is "dead."

Honor your feelings of reality when you dream of being with a deceased loved one.

You may have had the experience of dreaming of a departed loved one whose visit seemed *so real* that you felt differently the next morning, as if assured of their well-being, and thus better able to enjoy your own life again. Surely these are some of the most touching and beautiful dreams possible, when a beloved assures us that they are moving on to their next area of growth, and, so far from being extinguished, are happier than ever before. Does the dreammaker provide these for our own well-being and release from pain? Many therapists would say these dreams are part of the natural healing mechanism of the brain, which is trying to lessen the intensity of grief by providing hope of an afterlife. Others, myself included, would wonder if the connection of love is so great that we *are* able to communicate during the dream state, even across dimensions. None of us can answer that question for another. Trust your experience. If you feel and believe that you were with a loved one, or that a beloved came to visit you, then accept that. As you work with and recall your dreams more frequently, you will become attuned to the different qualities of feeling characteristic of different dreams, and you will be confident in trusting your own certainty. It is not at all uncommon to dream of someone fairly soon after their passing, and to hear assurances from them that they are not "dead" at all, and that there is in fact no death. These "death is only a doorway" dreams are dismissed by many as the mind's way of lessening our personal fear of death, while softening the blow of the loss of the loved one. Many people have had such dreams and do not speak about them because they naturally assume others would dismiss them, or find them odd or pathetic. Pay attention to your subjective sense of reality of the dream. Also pay attention to any lessening of your fear and grief. If your heart feels lighter in the morning, you may not quite understand what has happened, but you can trust that you have learned something significant, and that somehow things are not what you had assumed they were. While there is logic to the argument that the universality of these dreams points to our species' fear of death, it is also reasonable to wonder whether the universality of this phenomena is a clue to a broader view of what we define as "reality."

Lucid Dreams

Lucid dreams are those in which the dreamer is consciously aware of the dream state while still in it. Have you had the experience of going along, minding your own business, when something so extraordinary happens you are tipped off that you are in a dream? Often there is a sense of seeing through the action or events, and saying, "Wait a minute, this is a dream!" If you are an avid student of dreams then you *will* have this experience if you have not already. It seems the laws that govern dream action are not nearly so strict as were once believed. If you are involved in examining your dreams on a regular basis, you will tend to be more of a conscious participant in their production even while they are taking place. This is like the screen stars who act in *and* direct a film or television episode. This dual role is an exciting process, and is invaluable practice for the kind of versatility we need in waking reality.

Some therapists believe that seeing through our limitations is like becoming lucid in a dream, and realizing how often events are a matter of choice.

One type of lucid dream is the sort in which you are very active in the creation of the action. You will be quite aware that you are in the dream mode, and by choosing certain actions or activities you will be able to have things go in a certain direction. Here is a lucid dream that Nan shared with me.

> *I am building a house. I think that this is really going to be my "dream house," and then I realize that I am dreaming. I decide that I will have it exactly the way I would like it since I know I won't have to pay for it. I create just the environment I want, and enjoy myself immensely.*

Some researchers and counselors believe lucid dreams provide excellent opportunities to work out problems and challenges, as well as to explore as Nan did, creativity without limitations. Some workshops explore the ability to re-enter a dream imaginatively and to change the ending to suit yourself. There is something to be said for recognizing the dream state and deciding to confront your demons. I recently had this lucid dream confrontation:

> *I turn around and there is Kelly, my childhood friend. She is in many of my dreams, long after we ceased to know each other in waking life. I yell at*

her: "What are you doing in my dreams all the time? What do you want?" Kelly covers her face with her hands, and says, "I just want to be left alone."

Although I knew I was dreaming, I was not consciously controlling the action; rather I was participating in it with awareness. Kelly was a childhood friend, an extremely aggressive little girl, and in my dreams she represents the part of me that would like to take charge and get things done. The main part of my personality, a more self-effacing aspect, ironically tends to dominate the aggressive vital side of myself. Kelly comes into my dreams frequently to remind me of her existence and power for me as a resource. All too often though, I judge and criticize her instead of putting her to work. This dream alerted me to the fact that I have been "sitting on her" far too much lately.

Nan's dream, in which she is actively choreographing the action and events, and my own dream, in which I am aware of the dream state but surprised by the events, are two examples of lucid dreaming. If you are interested in cultivating this ability, you can do so by focusing on interpreting your other dreams, and by giving yourself the suggestion before sleep that you will become aware in your dreams. If you have the urge to re-run a dream and change it for yourself, you certainly can do so. Be sure to give yourself ample time with the original version though before you alter it. You need to fully understand the message and meaning of the dream as it was created for you before you adjust it to make yourself more comfortable. In a sense, such adjustments feel good, because we can create happy endings and easy transitions. If a dream makes you uncomfortable, remember that exaggerated feelings are part of the language of dreams, and are used to get your attention. If something is "hot" and charged for you, or frightens you, then you need to learn what's going on in the dream. After you understand the dynamics in your waking life that are showing through, feel free to alter things to move in the direction you desire.

Precognition and psychic dreams

Many people who remember their dreams, but know little about the way they work, are concerned that their nightmares will come true. How are you supposed to know when you receive a "warning," and when you are having a nightmare for other reasons? I was originally trained in a tradition that paid little attention to the possibility of precognition in dreams. In a sense, this is wise, for it is far more likely for someone to worry unnecessarily about the ominous qualities of a nightmare, and to essentially scare themselves, than it is for the dream to be a precognitive one. I cannot count the number of people who have come to me with nightmares; asking the burning question: "How do I know if this is a premonition?" This is a tough question. A few years ago, I would have recommended leaving the possibility of psychic information for your last pass at dream analysis. In other words, don't worry about that, except as a *remote* possibility. Since then, however, I have been made aware of so many precognitive dreams that I have had to reevaluate that opinion. Here is the precognitive dream of a good friend, who frequently has precognitive fragments in his dreams.

> *I am walking along a road minding my own business when several people chase me off the road. I run into the grassy meadow off to my left and am able to escape, but just barely. This seems very real and I recall it vividly when I awaken.*

The following day this man was walking along a road near his home when the following incident happened:

> "I saw that a pick-up truck coming down the road was slowly drifting off the road onto the shoulder and was heading straight toward me. I stopped, assuming the driver would steer back onto road, but he didn't. I took several steps down the grassy embankment on my left to get out of the way, but the truck kept coming at me! I jumped farther down the grassy slope and when I looked up I could see that the driver was asleep at the wheel.

The truck went off the shoulder right where I had been standing and started bouncing down the embankment. The driver woke when the truck started bouncing and pitching, and he was able to stop without his truck turning over."

After he had given his report to the police officers and was replaying the incident in his mind he suddenly remembered his dream from the night before.

Notice that my friend did not realize he'd had a precognitive dream until after the events of the following day. He said, however, "What was interesting is how calm I was throughout the entire incident. I sensed that something was unusual when the pick-up was several hundred feet away and did what I needed to do to avoid getting hit." So it is not necessary for you to decide which is a precognitive dream when it happens; your subconscious mind will be activated and prepared for whatever events transpire, regardless of your degree of recognition beforehand.

If you already know you tend to have precognitive dreams, because you so often experience their events later in your waking reality, then take that into account when doing your analysis. Certain people tend to have more precognitive dreams, while others apparently are less prone to them. The best way to know for sure is to keep a careful record.

One reason why the existence of precognitive dreams has been discounted by experts for so long is that your subconscious mind has such intense powers of perception that it can often accurately predict the future. Things you are unaware of consciously are pieced together by the subconscious and woven into dream messages that often "forecast" subsequent events. The combination of subliminal awareness and keen intuition, (unfettered by rationalizations) i*
an excellent problem-solver. This is exactly the type of *
sources your dreammaker uses to produce your dream*

I once worked for a company which merged *
wealthy and slightly nefarious individual in order to*
their cash-flow situation. I had reservations a* .
merger, because the individual moved in circl*
volved criminal as well as legitimate operation*
my worries though, because other co-worker*

my anxieties. When I had the following dream, I decided to trust my inner warnings and leave the firm.

> *We are selling firearms at the office. All of us have to wear ammunition belts, like Pancho Villa. We are told to pitch the arms over the phone to our customers. I can't believe we are doing this. It doesn't fit with what we stand for. But my boss is certain that we can make a lot of money this way, and that is what he cares about. I think to myself : "I don't want to be a part of this."*

I had a greater sense of certainty after this dream, that if criminal activities were not involved in our current business, at the very least ethical standards would take a turn for the worse in that company. I left the organization, and for a few weeks afterward, continued to have dream images of crime associated with the merger. Should events later transpire that mirror my dream images, it would be tempting to conclude that these were precognitive dreams; however I do not think that is the case. These were what I call *dream amalgamations*. The dreammaker selects and adds together dozens of little clues leading up to a conclusion. If you have ever watched Sherlock Holmes or Perry Mason finding clues and deducing the real situation behind the apparent mystery, you have seen this kind of talent at work. Your subconscious mind has this ability in great abundance. Because we are often busy "thinking" during our waking hours, and taking care of business, and because we frequently choose not to see what we don't wish to see, the waking mind will often miss conclusions that the dreaming mind catches and points out.

If you are dreaming of a current situation going badly, of a business opportunity being unsuccessful, of a lover betraying you, or of a danger to your health, *pay attention to the message.* Whether the dreammaker is utilizing psychic information, or whether you are experiencing a dream amalgamation, the critical point is the meaning of the dream.

Futuristic Visions

Dreams involving earthquakes, fire and flood are actually quite common. These images tend to appear in dreams during periods following personal turmoil. Individuals going through divorce or separation frequently process these changes as natural disasters during their sleep. Images of devastation, wreckage and loss depict the sense of emotional upheaval and struggle for survival (of well being) which often accompany drastic or unwanted change.

With the arrival of the twenty-first century an expectation of change seems to be part of our collective consciousness. The pace of contemporary life continues to escalate and increase individual and collective stress. Concerns regarding the survival of our species and planet have become legitimate and urgent topics of attention. I believe the majority of these dreams can be interpreted as personal metaphors utilizing contemporary symbols for loss and lack of control. However, many people ask me if they could possibly be getting a glimpse of the future.

I have collected a number of dreams in recent years dealing with global disasters, holocausts, and the end of the world. Although I don't believe these dreams are foretelling our future, I am intrigued whenever dreams contain themes shared by many people. In the majority of these cases there have been fairly clear connections between the dreamer's waking life conditions and the metaphoric level of the dreams. I had a number of similar dreams after the death of my father, and it is particularly common for children who have lost a parent to dream of global disasters at that time.

We don't yet have a full understanding of how dreams allow us to explore possibilities while we sleep. I suspect that one force behind our assorted dreams of disaster is our collective urge to prevent just the scenes our dreams depict. It may be that we are engaged in a vital process of exploring threats to our survival and experimenting with solutions. It's been my observation that some dreams do contain elements of the future. But they don't arise to announce doom and then leave us to our fate. Dreams of future events almost always provide greater choices and allow the dreamer to move toward or away from the events that have been witnessed. It seems likely that this function of activating choices operates as a general survival mechanism in all dreams. So any specter of the future whether global or personal could be considered a potential to be moved toward or avoided when we awaken.

If you have a dream you consider to be a futuristic vision you may wish to highlight the elements it contains, and make a special note of it in your dream journal. If the dream cannot be linked to a waking-life context in your present circumstances, and if it recurs often or appears to be "replayed" many times within one night, the chances of its containing non-ordinary information are increased.

Individuals who have highly unusual dream experiences often feel oppressed by their sense of having no one to talk to about them. This loneliness can be bleak and frightening when you are unsure how to interpret a bizarre event. I recommend that you make a point of finding someone with whom to share these experiences. Although you may not find satisfactory conclusions or tidy understandings, you will find greater confidence and peace of mind by being able to share and sort through your dreams and your thoughts about them.

Chapter 9

"Dear Dreammaker..." Your Nightly Advice Column

With all the advice dreams have to offer you, as well as presenting the inside scoop on what is really going on in your life, is it possible to ask your dreams for guidance about a problem or question you have? It certainly is possible, and many people have found it enormously helpful to do so.

If you are faced with a decision, or feel you are not creating the result you want, you are in an excellent position to ask for some help from your dreams. If you are just beginning to work with dreams, you may be hesitant to ask for dreams about certain subjects. Don't worry. This service is free! You have the best guide/mentor/counselor possible at your disposal.

Your dreammaker *has no other job* than to do everything possible to help you out. Be respectful, but don't be shy when it comes to asking for what you need to know. One word of caution: Don't become agitated or feel like a failure if you don't have dreams that spell out the course of action you are supposed to take. You aren't visiting the Oracle at Delphi—you are asking the deeper layers of your mind to give you some input, and you may not get a response you understand or recognize right away. If the input is important to you, be persistent and scrupulous about recording and examining your dreams. You may want to write out a question before you go to sleep, and write the dreams you receive upon awakening. Or you may simply go to sleep repeating the question over and over to yourself as you drift off.

When I was searching for a graduate psychology program, I asked for dream help in deciding whether to join a residential program, or whether to venture into a more appealing but rather controversial off-campus program where the students can design more of their own coursework. I had the following dream:

> *I am driving on the freeway, going as fast as I can, but I don't know where I am or where I am going. I am just in a big hurry. I don't have a map. I can't believe that I took off for unknown territory without a map. I have a sense of urgency, but I really don't know where I am supposed to be, if I am on course or what. This isn't going to do me any good without a map.*

I realized immediately that my sense of self-direction was giving me a lot of fuel to pursue my education and goals, but that driving urgently without direction wasn't going to get me anywhere. How would I know if I was "on course," without any guidelines? How would I know when I had arrived? I sensed that although my introversion caused me to always want to do things on my own, this particular trip was one in which I would need help and guidance. "The freeway" wouldn't be the best way in this case. I decided on a school that offered me the leeway to explore many of the more exciting and experimental contemporary areas of psychology, but which also provided a great deal of support and grounding in the areas needed for licensing and modern practice.

When you are asking a dream for guidance, it will be easiest if you ask rather directly for what you need to know. If you get too esoteric in your wording, you may receive a dream that is just as confusing as your question. Just ask, as you would a friend: "What do I need to know about Harry, before I move in with him?" Or, "What will happen if I take this job?" Or, "What am I overlooking in the way I'm handling my son?"

Here is the dream of a young businessman named Terry, who was wondering whether to accept a new position with a different company. He asked before going to sleep: "What will happen if I take the job?"

> *I go to make a phone call, and find that I have tons of paper money in my pocket. No change though. I go into a store to get some change. I have so much money I can't believe it, but when I take it out of my pocket, it doesn't look like real money; it's play money, like monopoly money. They won't give me change at the counter, but I don't care. I'm rich. I go somewhere else to get something and they won't take the play money either. People are so silly. I am ex-*

cited though. I have never had so much money. I just laugh and I leave the store.

Unfortunately, Terry interpreted this dream to mean that if he took the new job, he would get rich, because in the dream he *felt* rich. He didn't wonder until much later about the fact that the money in his pockets was *play* money. It wasn't real and couldn't be used for anything. Terry took the job, and the company went under, still owing him compensation that he never recovered. In this case Terry's dreammaker knew that the riches being promised were illusory. Terry would get the *feeling* of being rich for awhile, but he would be unable to trade with the currency he got from that job. Had Terry scrutinized the dream a bit more closely, he might have saved himself some hard work and trouble.

Be careful and objective with the dream input you receive as a result of your questions. You need not do something that is suggested in a dream if it doesn't seem wholesome or correct to you. But treat the insights you receive as the invaluable resource they are. If you have a dream you don't fully understand, but sense it is important for you, ask others what they think of it. Don't assume they will have the answers, but pay attention to their ideas and see if anything seems on target. Do some reading about dreams and see if you don't "stumble" upon something that makes your own dream click for you. Your subconscious is enormously perceptive and can help you to discover exactly what you're seeking when you are clear about your intention to learn.

Some people have amazing results with incubating dreams right away while others find their results more subtle and varied in success. Because there are such individual differences with this process, be prepared to experiment a bit with it and learn what is most comfortable, effective and easy for you. Some people have good luck by introducing a subject that is compelling for them at the moment and letting their dreammaker construct a dream for them. I find the more definite the question I ask, the more succinct is the answering dream. If you are prone to nightmares, you can try asking for more soothing and clarifying dreams when you awaken. Many of my students are able to have dreams that address the same issues as their nightmare, but with less drama and fear by simply asking for that kind of support as they drift back to sleep. This reduces the chances of falling back into a bad dream by letting your dreammaker know: "Hey, all right, you have my attention and I'm listening! Now could you please send me that information again without scaring me to death?" The next dream that comes is often recognizable as a less formidable exploration of the same subject and feelings.

Occasionally you may ask for guidance from your dreams, and then find that you can't remember them. (It happens.) Don't worry. There is no limit on the number of times you get to ask a question. You may already have had the experience of wondering what to do about something as you go to bed, and in the morning having such a definite sense of direction that you know exactly what you are going to do. You have very likely sorted out the issue in your dreams, and even though you don't consciously recall the details, you will bring with you the sense of resolution you achieved. It is a time-honored tradition to "sleep on it" when you need to make a decision. Most of us intuitively know that we will be better able to address an important issue when we are rested and the mind is fresh. No small part of this ability to "know" what to do in the morning comes from the sorting and double-checking that goes on in our dreams. It is not always necessary to recall a dream if you awaken with a strong sense of certainty. Don't be afraid to be satisfied with your own knowing.

Finally, feel free to ask for dreams to show you anything you need to know right now. They will anyway, but it is nice to have an easy rapport between your thinking self and your dreammaker. I frequently ask for direction with spiritual and ethical questions, and ask for advice on making the best possible contribution with my professional activities. If you receive a dream you are not able to fully decipher, ask for another dream to clarify the message. This is like asking for a composer's "variations on a theme." If you are not certain you understand, but you sense it is important, stick with it until you get a dream that means something to you.

Chapter 10

Sharing Dreams with Others

More and more people around the world are discovering the rewards of sharing dreams in groups. I'm often contacted by people who want to know how to get a dream group started, or where to find one in their area. You may have noticed that reading this book gave you a sense that you aren't alone and your sense of the importance of dreams is valid. That feeling of support and sanity is even greater when you have regular friends with whom you can share dreams and explore their significance.

Finding A Dream Group

Many towns have a special kind of local paper that is focused on events, entertainment and "what's happening" around town. Many people don't look at such papers because they're very trendy looking and seem to be for the single, active crowd. But take a look inside and you may see a listing of classes, workshops, lectures and book signings. This is often where a new dream group will be advertised, or someone in your area who works with dreams will list their services.

You may also have a local bookstore that caters to self-help, recovery and personal growth events. Browse through their bulletin boards, read their newsletter and even ask the store personnel if they know of anyone working with dreams in your area.

If there is a community college in your area, check their catalog for adult education classes. Many community colleges love offering dream analysis classes and sponsoring groups because they've become in demand in recent years. If there is nothing in their catalog and you feel comfortable with. try a bit of detective work. Consider calling their psychology or social science department and find out who might have an idea of someone in your area who works with dream analysis.

Community centers sometimes sponsor dream groups too, and the rates are inexpensive. Check periodically through their catalogs, and if they don't have a dream class yet, drop the coordinator a note saying you'd love to see one in their next line up. Coordinators keep a list of qualified instructors on file and will often try to get a class together in response to requests from the public.

Many churches also offer brief courses in working with dreams. If your church is open to personal growth topics and encourages group activities suggest to the activities planner that they include a course in dreams in their next schedule of events. Most of the sources I mentioned are thrilled when people suggest classes to them, so I encourage you to be vocal about what you're looking for, and tell your friends with similar interests to keep their eyes open for you as well.

Starting A Dream Group

If you can't find what you're looking for in your area, or don't feel comfortable with the ideology or methods of the group you have located, you may want to start a group of your own. This isn't as far-fetched as you might think. If you have a few friends who share your interest in dreams you can suggest meeting regularly to discuss them. The beauty of this plan is that you can all decide how often you want to get together, and whether to meet always in the same place or trade off so that each person has a turn having the group at her home.

The home-based dream group is becoming popular around the world because it is very like an extended family and provides a chance to learn from others and get different view-points on a dream. In most cases there is no charge for these meetings and no advertising. Most groups allow members to invite serious-minded friends to join, but "drop in" guests are not encouraged since the discussions are somewhat personal. After you have a group of friends together, the expectations and preferences for the group can explored so that everyone understands and feels comfortable.

If you participate in a support or discussion group now, you may want to suggest to them that dream discussions would be an enriching area to include in the group. I am frequently invited by groups to come and teach them about dreams for a few weeks so that they can include dream work in their discussions in the future.

If you don't know enough people who share an interest in dreams, consider launching a group through your school, church, club, or community center. By volunteering to coordinate and facilitate a peer dream group for several weeks, you can meet people who are fascinated with dreams and develop enough acquaintances to then continue with a smaller group that is more ongoing. Although this may sound like a lot of work, or an exotic tangent, the rewards of having a group of people with whom you share your dreams is truly immeasurable. Particularly if you are a vivid dreamer, you will find that having a forum for discussing dreams is enormously rewarding and great source of stability in your life.

Suggestions for Sharing Dreams in Groups

There are many different ways to work with dreams, to process the feelings they stir and probe the layers of imagery they present. Here are a few general guidelines that seem universally supportive:

- **Find out which members brought a dream hoping to share it at that meeting.** If there are too many dreams to work with at that meeting, find out whose need is most urgent and who feels strongly that they need the groups help. Ideally members can take turns sharing dreams, but most people feel fine about giving extra attention where needed as long as no one takes advantage of this flexibility.
- **When someone is about to share a dream, ask first if there is any background information the group should know before they hear the dream.** Unless this question is asked up front, there is a tendency for people to forget to share relevant information until you have

been working with the dream for some time. If the dreamer received a call from his brother-in-law demanding money, and that night dreamed about con men, this is may be relevant to the discussion.

- **Allow the dreamer to recount the dream fully before asking any questions.** You want the dreamer to feel and "be inside" the dream again during the process of telling it. If you get confused by a change of scene and blurt out "*what* building?" in the midst of the story, that connection is burst like a bubble. The remainder of the telling will likely be flat, self-conscious and without the subjective connection that helps the group work be accurate. Bite your tongue and jot down your question, you'll be able to get clarification in a moment.

- **Direct questions first to aspects of the dream that need clarification.** Before trying to decipher a dream, make sure you are clear about what happened. If the dreamer was hanging upside down, giving birth, or flying by flapping their arms, get a mental picture that matches their own before going on.

- **Ask about the feelings and experiences within the dream before "jumping" to questions about waking life.** Even if you feel certain you know what the dream is about, hold back for awhile to allow the group to explore the dream and flesh out areas that seem mysterious. If the dream included a dark vampire, you might ask whether this was a creepy vampire or a seductive one. These distinctions are vital and can be neglected if you don't invite the dreamer to clarify them.

- **Ask if the dreamer has made any associations or interpretations about their dream.** This question should be formed shortly after the dream is shared, however I find that it launches the interpretive phase of the process. If the dream has not yet been clarified for everyone, you then have some people wrapping up their conclusions about the interpretation while others are still asking "where did the gunfighter come from?" When someone has shared a dream and their story is followed by a prolonged silence, this can be an ideal time to check whether they have any insights about the dream already. I frequently ask "where are you with this dream, have you made any connections to it?" or "do you have any sense about this dream so far?" It is helpful to ask this early on because many people are shy when it comes to presenting their own thoughts about their dream. Often the observations made in response to this question are not exactly the same as the interpretations that will eventually emerge. But anything the dreamer says at this point is relevant, because these are the thoughts and feelings catalyzed by the dream.

- **Allow the dreamer to maintain control of the process.** Sometimes dream work is so exciting that people get on a roll with their interpretation and overlook the fact that the dreamer obviously does not agree. While it is possible to be so unaware of a dream's meaning that you don't "get it" when it's suggested to you, my observation is that when a dreamer feels the group or an interpretation is off track they are usually right. Use the dreamer's reactions as your tuning fork and respect them absolutely. Do not suggest the dreamer is in denial or doesn't want to hear the truth. If you get into territory that isn't clicking for the dreamer but makes sense to you, then you may have tapped into something in her dream that you identify with. This is a common occurrence in group work, and when it happens just acknowledge it by saying: "I may be projecting my own issues here, because I can relate to some of this dream." This acknowledgement is magic. It snaps the group back to more fruitful explorations, and it encourages all the group members to "stay honest" about the tendency toward and value of projections.

- **Use contrast to make a point.** The experiences in our dreams may seem hazy until we are offered an explanation that contradicts our experience. For this reason, it is easier to elicit details from dreamers by suggesting absurd or opposite feelings to them. The person who dreamed of a hairy spider on their bedspread may shrug and say, "it was just there," when asked about it. You can try and guess all day long how they felt about it, but if you say: "Did you want to play with the spider?" they will probably connect with their feelings and retort "good heavens no! I wanted to kill it but was so scared I couldn't move." It may sound silly to investigate a mystery by asking questions you believe to be wrong, but this is a wonderful way to let the dreamer discover and articulate their feelings without interrogating them for an extended time, or making them feel inept by asking them to be more specific.

- **Realize the dreamer is in a special state when sharing.** When group dream work is in progress, the dreamer is in an altered state. They may look normal, but they are half in the room with you and half in the dream. This makes them very vulnerable, sometimes emotional, and more easily "lost" amidst rapid-fired debating. They need to be asked questions rather than "told" about their dream, and they need to be prompted by requests that permit them to retrieve small details or define their experience. Heady philosophical questions or references to theories are not going to make much sense to them at this time. The dreamer should be considered the one who knows best when the group is on target.

- **Suspend your conversational style and pace.** When you ask a question of a dreamer or another group member, it may take an unusually long time for them to formulate a response. Grit your teeth and allow them to locate the information and put it into words. When the tension and fun of a dream exploration is underway this is particularly hard for some of us to tolerate. But it is vital. When a question is asked of a dreamer, wait. Let them answer. Don't jump in. This style is drastically different from conversations with friends where you finish their sentence for them or disagree and blurt out just what you think. Because dream work can be very intimate and personal, many people find themselves slipping into their most informal conversational style since they feel so close and caring toward group members. By being on the lookout for this tendency, you can help prevent it from short-changing the dreamer who needs pauses in the process to access information.

- **When the discussion of a dream feels complete, ask for ideas from the dreamer, or the group about the useful insights that have emerged.** Sometimes even if the interpretation of a dream is only partial, but you've done all you can with it for this session, it is still possible to recognize what may be useful about it.

- **Keep track of a reasonable distribution of time, or have assign someone each meeting to keep the focus**

equitable. Some groups will use a timer to keep the work on a single dream equal, say 15 minutes to half an hour per dream. Some groups are quite strict about keeping time, others prefer to address each dream until they feel satisfied about the interpretation.

- **Allow the dreamer to say thank you, acknowledge what she's learned, and close the discussion of her dream.** In a way dreamwork is like a dance. The dreamer provides the impulse by sharing a dream and the group then dances and explores it. When this process has gone as far as it can fruitfully go or as far as time allows, the dream should then be psychically returned to it's rightful owner. By allowing the dreamer the last word and the closing of the work on her own dream, it is a way for her to reclaim ownership of the experience and say out loud what has been useful or thought-provoking about the work. Even if she only says, "wow, that's given me a lot to think about, I'm glad we did this," she has resumed control and received the experience. This doesn't mean that only the dreamer will know when the process is finished for that session. Typically the group will become aware that a dream has been "solved" or the work is done for this session. By making this format a traditional part of the group style, it also permits the dreamer to close the discussion if she feels tired, unable to go on for any reason, or if she has made a connection that she wishes to think about privately rather than bring into the group.

The details of how your group operates best and the needs of its members will emerge naturally over time. In the beginning it is helpful to have more "rules" and guidelines in place. The longer a group meets, the less necessary formal guidelines become, since the effectiveness of the process and the enjoyment of the members becomes the measurement of what works best for you.

Helping Friends and Family with Dreams

If you become involved in working with a dream group, or tell many people about your interest in dreams, you may soon become labeled as the informal dream expert in your family, social circle or at the workplace. People will tell you their dreams in the oddest situations, ask you questions at parties and want you to interpret dreams when they meet you at the water cooler. The hunger to have someone listen to a vivid dream is intense and the yearning to connect with the meaning of a dream is both compelling and natural. The inappropriate and sometimes silly ways people react to this hunger shouldn't discourage or embarrass you. Modern culture has only recently given the official green light to discussing dreams, and many of us want to get the answers without having any clue as to how to ask the questions. To help you cope with this phenomenon if it happens to you, here are some suggestions which may help.

Telling a Dream is its own Reward

For most people, telling their dream to someone who actually wants to hear it is sheer heaven. Listening with interest is a gift you can easily give that helps the other person even if neither of you says a word about what the dream might mean. It can be odd to hear a dream that is obviously important and then have the person chalk it up to the full moon or the spicy food they ate. But when a dream story is followed immediately by an explanation that dismisses the dream from relevance, you have just been told between the lines that this person doesn't want to hear about what their dream means, they just wanted to tell you about it. It is always a good idea to respect the person's signals and thank them for sharing such an amazing dream with you. The next time this person has a provocative dream they may want to find out something more about it, but not this time. By becoming known as someone who loves to hear dreams and study them you will encourage everyone you know to think about their dreams in a different way, whether or not you ever say anything convincing to them.

Don't Volunteer an Interpretation

You may be tempted to point out something about a dream that strikes you as familiar or obvious. But unless the person in question asks you to do so, your comments are really an invasion of their privacy. When someone tells you a dream, they often have no idea that you will see things about their history, their sex life, their insecurities and private thoughts. *They* think they are telling you about this weird and kooky dream. To then jump into the meaning you perceive violates the unspoken contract you have with the other person, who never agreed to discuss that level of the dream's contents. When someone shares a dream, thank them and comment about its vividness, creativity, or some other objective quality. This gracefully rewards them, honors the exchange you've had and sets the stage for either closing the discussion or allowing them to ask for your ideas about the dream.

Respond Cautiously and Gently to Requests for Interpretation

When someone truly wants to know about the meaning of a dream, there are certain hallmarks of genuine interest, permission to explore and readiness to learn. If these hallmarks aren't there, it's reasonable to assume their interest is mere curiosity, making conversation, or even teasing. In that case your response should match *that* level of conversation by being polite, friendly and sometimes affectionately dismissive. Here are the hallmarks of a more serious question:

- The dreamer and you are usually alone or able to speak with some degree of privacy.
- There is adequate time for an extended conversation of a least a few minutes.
- Your physical surroundings permit conversation; you can sit, make eye contact, and hear without difficulty.
- The dreamer may ask you formally if you have time to discuss a dream they've had. When you agree that you have time they will then tell you the dream or ask their

question. (This brief permission-asking is the single most important hallmark of genuine interest in a dream.)

- When you begin to speak about their dream, the person will look at you and listen. If they look away, interrupt, or shout across the room at someone else, they may not be interested or ready to look at the dream after all. Many people don't realize they don't want to get into a dream until someone addresses it with obvious seriousness and insight. If the person withdraws, let them do so gracefully and don't be offended.

- The person may tell you a dream, and then ask if it "means" a particular thing that they are worried about. In most cases, this shows they have given the dream enough thought to start trying to make sense of it, and are in the process of considering and discarding possible explanations. It is appropriate to reassure them about their concern and comment briefly if you have an idea about what their dream suggests.

- If someone tells you a dream and then says "why would I dream something like that?" They probably have a very mild but genuine interest in the answer.

Typically when someone is genuinely interested in learning about a dream some if not all of these hallmarks will be present. If someone asks you about a dream in a situation that doesn't permit you to discuss it you can be fairly sure that they don't really want to know about it. *This is true even if they ask you to interpret their dream.* They have set the stage to make it impossible to do this, while at the same time asking for your help. The more skillful you get at gracefully handling these moments the more control you'll have over your time, and your serious exploration of dreams will be less be contaminated by irreverent humor or absurd encounters.

Give General Interpretations and Suggestions

People tend to think dreams are interpreted in the same way tea leaves are read, or fortunes told. They may present a dream with obvious hopes that you will explain it completely and shed light on their future as well. Don't feel obliged to try and match those expectations. You can help them by sharing your previous experiences with similar dreams or imagery if you have them, or by suggesting how to explore a symbol and discover their own associations to it. If you do have a strong sense of a dream and they seem ready and interested to hear it, then share your ideas. It is both empowering and accurate to caution them that this is merely your impression and if it is right it should strike a chord with them or fit their experience. This is simply common sense and everyone can understand this principle when it is pointed out to them. This way you've answered their question, given them your sense of the dream, and educated them a bit about how to evaluate what you've suggested. General (rather than specific) comments seem to allow people to recognize where there is a match with their experience and make the bridge to their waking life them-selves. This is much more efficient than trying to "guess" what life situation they might be going through, or to provide an in-depth interpretation on the spot.

Be Fearless and Encouraging

Don't be afraid to enter discussions about dreams or to help people who seem sincere. As long as you are candid about the exploratory nature of dream interpretation and encourage others to draw their own conclusions, you are on the right track. You'll have a few odd conversations, and learn who among your co-workers and relatives is not ready to talk about dreams. Some people find the topic oddly provocative, and even shocking. Don't feel obliged to convert or educate those who aren't interested. Do encourage those who are intrigued to read about the topic and explore the subject in whatever way draws them. By discussing and encouraging a relationship with the dreaming mind you do everyone around you a service. The truths our dreams contain are predisposed to come forth once we turn our attention toward them with an open heart. The skill of interpreting dreams is quite easy in comparison to the larger "trick" of giving ourselves and each other permission to explore this wonderful landscape.

Great times to ask for special help from your dreams.

♦ When you have mixed feelings about a relationship and want greater clarity.

♦ When you're efforts to accomplish a goal don't work no matter what you try.

♦ When you "should" want one thing, but feel drawn to another choice.

♦ When you wonder why your reaction to a minor event was unusually strong.

♦ When you need to understand how to get through to someone.

♦ When you long to view a problem from a higher perspective but aren't sure how to get there.

♦ When you feel that part of you knows the answer, but it is just on the other side of a veil.

Chapter 11

What to Expect
From Here

As you continue to recall and work with dreams regularly, you will frequently find upon awakening that both a dream and its meaning are quite clear to you. Even when you "know" what a dream means you will be able to learn still more by recording it. The more experienced with dream language you become the less time it will take for you to arrive at an interpretation. The act of recording or sharing a dream sometimes allows its meaning to come clear. It is natural for your interest in dreamwork to fluctuate. People often become quite busy and "forget" or drift away from their regular dream analysis for a time. Don't be dismayed or feel guilty if you observe this in yourself. The passage of time can enhance your ability to understand dreams, even when you have neglected to focus upon them.

If you are going through a transition such as divorce, job change, a period of intense personal growth, or a grieving process, you can especially benefit from a regular habit of dream interpretation. Your dreams work very effectively to help you negotiate the challenges and pitfalls of life. If you are going through a difficult or confusing time, you will be assisted and support greatly if you can make the time to attend to your internal process.

Dreams help to resolve
"unresolvable" differences

One difference between the dream state and the waking state is that in dreams the pattern of opposites doesn't hold true. You may be in one room and simultaneously in another. You can be both male and female. You can be any race—you can fly, swim, and walk. You can be talking to someone, and then *become* the other person listening to you. The boundaries, separations, and black-and-white thinking which define so much of our waking experience are suspended (or revealed as illusory) in the dream state.

I believe much of the stress and pain we experience in life is connected with our insistence upon viewing things as either "good" or "evil," either one way, or the other. I am not suggesting that many of these evaluations are not *accurate* assessments, but that the process of coding experience and perception in this way is a style of thinking which creates stress, pain, and confusion. By viewing our world as sets of opposites, we limit the possibilities for connectedness and insure that for every profit, we shall feel a loss. Many of the worlds great religions, and now some contemporary therapies and meditations teach practitioners to follow regimens which permit moments of "transcendence" in which the separations between things are recognized as illusory, and a pleasurable, healing sense of unity and connectedness is experienced.

One function of dreams then, may be to provide experiences each night in which the rigid rules of existence that contain us during waking hours are suspended. Bridges are formed between one belief and another, one possible self and another, between humans and animals, and between what we conceptualize as life and death. It may be that we need this respite from waking distinctions and evaluations—that in fact, the very bizarreness of our dreams is a purposeful mental-health-treatment helping enable us to bear the apparent separation we experience during the day.

Working with your dreams will assist you in seeing the connections between things in your waking life. You will understand much more about why people do the things they do, and you will become more comfortable with diversity and differences of all kinds, in others as well as in yourself.

You will feel that you have better "instincts" or intuition

After a time, people who make a habit of working with dreams appear to develop tremendously good powers of intuition. A part of intuition is simply permitting yourself to listen to what you believe to be true, even when you have no evidence to support it. Because more information appears in dreams than you would be aware of consciously, you will have access to far more information than you possessed before you explored your dreams. This additional information would have overloaded you during your waking hours and made it difficult for you to concentrate and get things done. During sleep, however, relevant chunks of information are incorporated into dream action and experiences, so that in a sense, you will be shown far more than you realized you knew. At times the revelations in your dreams will be so astounding and accurate that it will seem as if they came from an outside source. As time passes, you will develop a "feel" for these kind of revelations and will appreciate them as marvelous, but not unusual, occurrences.

You will come to recognize your talents, abilities, and personal power to a greater degree

For many, growing up is an obstacle course that keeps them busy just trying not to bungle opportunities or "make the wrong choice." Life is fast-paced today, with myriad pressures and rapid changes. It is often only after several passages and experiences that we notice the ache of unfulfilled potential, or the quiet yearning for activities we neglected because they appeared impractical or without tangible reward. It is a shock to some to realize that though they stopped writing, painting, dancing, or acting years ago, their psyche still remembers and considers these gifts important. A secretary who was unable to attend college as a girl may dream of a long conversation with Albert Einstein encouraging her to take night classes. An overweight former athlete who became a successful attorney may dream of leading calisthenics classes and feeling fit again. A budding writer may dream of nursing a sick author back to health. Someone who longs to study for the ministry may dream of taking long walks with Billy Graham.

If you dream of someone famous who is known for their profession, talent, or contribution, and you don't know anyone in waking life who reminds you of the celebrity, it is highly likely that they are representing that talent as it exists in *you*. This is not to suggest that you sell your home and move to an island to become a painter—but it is likely that you would be more balanced, healthy, and fulfilled, and the unknown hunger haunting you would be assuaged by allowing that aspect of yourself to be a greater part of your waking experience. If the celebrity in the dream is wounded, dead, or starving, that is likely informing you that you have all but "killed off" that aspect of yourself. However, it is never too late. You can, more easily than you realize, incorporate into your waking life the kinds of activities that would stimulate and enliven that part of yourself. A good point to remember is this: If you find yourself thinking about your heart's desire in terms of yes or no, then broaden your spectrum of possibilities. You needn't deny yourself your deepest desire totally nor quit your job to start your own business. You can stay where you are and tiptoe into the water, giving yourself the experiences you crave without destroying your current life-style.

If you tend to doubt your own power, or identify yourself in a limited way, dreams will be presented to you which reveal you in a more powerful and capable light. Power is a touchy issue. It tends to be something we all desire, but at the same time we deny the existence of the power we have inside. In a sense we are all like the characters in the *Wizard of Oz* story (the Lion, the Scarecrow, and the Tin Man), searching outside ourselves for some oracle to bestow upon us the strengths we secretly possess but cannot acknowledge we have. If you dream of yourself suddenly vanquishing a dragon, or flying freely over traffic, or of commanding barriers to dissolve, pay attention to those images. You are being shown a far more genuine picture of yourself than you realize.

In a very real sense, embracing your dreams allows you to embrace your own power and capacity to grow and create. I encourage you to begin to *doubt* your previous doubts about yourself, and to claim as your own the heroic characters who often appear in your dreams. I believe you may find that in life as well as in dreams, *you are* the hero you have been waiting for.

Chapter Notes & References

Chapter 1   "I Wonder What That Dream Meant"

Gayle Delaney, *Living Your Dreams*, Harper & Rowe, 1981. p. 136 "The Many Faces of Inspiration." Inspirational dreams are described by some as sensations of "pure knowing." These dreams may be difficult to recall, and difficult to analyze because so much of their content is intangible.

Patricia Garfield, *Creative Dreaming*, Ballantine Books, 1974, p.199. Garfield suggests that dream imagery is important in and of itself, and can be used for purposes of meditation, self-direction and personal growth.

Chapter 2   Adjust Your Lens to See What is There

June Singer, "A Jungian Approach to Dreamwork" *Dreamtime and Dreamwork: Decoding the Language of the Night* edited by Stanley Krippner, Jeremy Tarcher/Perigee 1990, p.64. Singer contends that dreams are created holistically rather than piecemeal as our conscious thought processes tend to deal with information. She calls this unconscious process a kind of "diffuse attention." Details invisible to the conscious mind are actually quite clear to the unconscious.

Jeremy Taylor, *Where People Fly and Water Runs Uphill*, Warner Books, 1993, Chapter 1, "What You Should Know About Dreams: Ten Basic Assumptions." pp. 3-11. Taylor suggests that "all dreams come in the service of health and wholeness, and that only the dreamer can say with certainty what meaning his or her dream contains.

Gayle Delaney, *Living Your Dreams*, Harper & Rowe, 1981, p. 5. Delaney provided dreamworkers with an invaluable metaphor when she suggested that we each conceive of dreams as "productions," and described dream elements as "characters" "setting" "props" and "action." This analogy provided a turning point in the way I conceptualize dreams and the elements within them.

Chapter 3   Your Dream Journal: A Tool For Remembering

Ann Faraday, *The Dream Game*, AFAR Publishers, 1974, Chapter 3, "Keeping a Dream Diary" pp. 37-48. Faraday encourages students of dreams to keep a diary of their dreams, and to record all dream material they manage to catch: considering no fragment too small, no nuance too trivial to note. She also suggests capturing as many dreams as possible during each night.

Chapter 4   Dream Language

Louis Mehl, *Mind and Matter*, Mindbody Press, discussion of symbolization p.106. Mehl, a wholistic physician describes the mind's ability to create symbols for illness, health, and aspects of the self.

Ann Faraday, *The Dream Game*, AFAR Publishers, "Why the

Universal Language Has No Dictionary," pp. 51-66. Faraday expresses aptly the current belief among dreamworkers that dream images are designed to reveal rather than conceal meaning, thus what may seem a bizarre image is in fact a poetic gestalt of feeling, action, and subjective lived experience which is almost mathematically perfect in symbolizing that which it depicts. The bizarreness lies in the confines of the perspective through which we view the symbol, not in the symbol itself.

Chapter 5   The 5-Step Technique

Gayle Delaney, *Breakthrough Dreaming: How to Tap the Power of Your 24-Hour Mind*, Bantam Books, 1991, "Unlocking The Secrets of Your Dreams," pp. 46-75. Delaney explains the importance of bringing an attitude of humor mixed with reverence to your dreamwork, and offers marvelous suggestions on diagramming dreams and working with outlines of their major elements.

Jeremy Taylor, *Where People Fly and Water Runs Uphill*, Warner Books, 1993, Appendix II, Some Basic Hints for Working With Your Dreams by Yourself. pp. 263-268. Taylor suggests creative approaches for "breaking into" those dreams which are especially difficult to understand. Suggestions include drawing the dream, acting out the action of the dream, and creating a truncated version of the dream consisting of its emotional elements.

Chapter 6   Typical Symbols and Metaphors

Patricia Garfield, *Women's Bodies, Women's Dreams*, Ballantine Books, 1988, "Women's Sexual Dreams" pp. 118-136. Garfield shares dream examples of snakes, beds, phallic-shaped objects, and aggressive animals as symbols of masculine energy and sexual themes.

Robert H. Hopcke, *Men's Dreams, Men's Healing*, Shambhala, 1990, "The Dream of the Adolescent Cop," pp. 41-74. Hopcke, a Jungian analyst who specializes in working with men and men's dreams, offers insight into the action-oriented themes within men's dreams, as well as their issues with authority and autonomy (sometimes depicted in dream imagery by policemen and other authority figures.)

Patricia Garfield, *The Healing Power of Dreams*, " Simon & Schuster 1992, Forewarning and Diagnostic Dreams" pp. 86-114. Garfield has an uncanny knack for recognizing physical metaphors and symbology within dreams. She offers invaluable guidelines for learning to distinguish between physical warning signs in dreams and symbolic elements which have psychological, but not physical meaning.

Louise L. Hay, *You Can Heal Your Life*, Hay House, Inc., 1984, 150-188, Hay, a counselor and teacher offers a list of body parts, illnesses and their psychological connections and probable symbolic meanings gleaned from decades of experience working with chronically and terminally ill patients.

Zev Wanderer, and Tracy Cabot, *Letting Go: a 12-week Personal Action Program to Overcome a Broken Heart.* "Broken hearts" are one of the most common of dream issues to arise on a recurring basis, and to re-emerge upon the anniversary of a break-up or death. Wanderer and Cabot dissect relationship fears with a precision and clarity that assists the reader in recognizing the shape of personal fears and the manner in which those fears create a denial of the potential for love.

Chapter 6   **Extraordinary Dreams**

Gayle Delaney, *Breakthrough Dreaming,* Bantam Books, 1991, "Nightmares, Recurring Dreams, and Common Dream Themes," pp. 353-378. Delaney discusses common nightmares, and common themes.

Joan Windsor, *The Inner Eye: Your Dreams Can Make You Psychic,* Prentice-Hall 1985, pp. "Dream Interpretation," 115-122. Windsor provides helpful suggestions on interpreting dreams which seem to contain transpersonal themes; accepting possibilities and checking for connections to life issues.

Stanley Krippner, *Dreamtime and Dreamwork,* "Tribal Shamans and Their Travels into Dreamtime, pp.185-193. Krippner suggests we note the openness of native peoples in accepting the impact and "reality" of their dream experiences. If something occurred in sleep, "that action was considered to be, in some sense, real." This is a helpful construct for the dream enthusiast to try on for size: if you live through a dreamed experience, you are in a sense different than you were before. For the purposes of personal growth and self-exploration the sooner dreamers can begin to respect dreams as having "a reality" the faster and deeper the rewards of their dreamwork will become.

Melvin Morse, *Closer to The Light,* Villard Books, 1990, "The Pure Light" pp. 115-134. Morse, a pediatrician well known for his exploration of the near-death-experience among children, describes their universal description of pure, transformative light, which not only illuminates but conducts emotions (of love) as well. This description of light is also prevalent among dreamers (who recall dreams of light). The student searching for possible explanations/connections regarding light dreams may wish to refer to Morse's material.

Michael Talbot, *The Holographic Universe,* Harper Collins Publishers, 1992, pp. 1-50, 206, 209-10. Talbot discusses the holographic model of consciousness, and the possibility that the universe functions from a holographic model. He suggests this as an explanation for such phenomena as telepathy, pre-cognition, and the continual pattern of reality replicating our thoughts and beliefs.

Jon Klimo, *Channeling: Investigations on Receiving Information From Paranormal Sources,* Jeremy Tarcher, Inc. 1987, Dream Channeling, pp. 185-204. Klimo discusses possible reasons why the dream state can be a source of such unusual material. In some ways the dream state is similar to the trance state of psychics or meditators, and "the dreaming self seems more receptive to anomalous communication than the waking self...." Klimo believes people who dream of receiving information from another and find that the information received is indeed beyond what they could have "normally" known, may want to trust in their experience—using common sense and personal intuition as benchmarks for credence.

Stephen LaBerge, *Lucid Dreaming*, Ballantine, 1985, The Practical Dreamer: Applications of Lucid Dreaming, pp.167-196. LaBerge describes a "Healing Dream" in which lucid interaction with dream imagery acts as a catalyst for healing.

Chapter 7   Dear Dreammaker...Your Nightly Advice Column

Gayle Delaney, *Living Your Dreams*, Harper & Rowe, 1979, pp. 20-32. Delaney advocates the use of a "dream focusing phrase" prior to falling asleep as a method for inducing dreams on certain topics or questions.

Ann Faraday, *The Dream Game*, AFAR Publishers, 1974, Asking Your Dreams For Help, pp. 142-168. Faraday suggests writing a comprehensive request in paragraph form to the inner mind or "dream power" prior to going to sleep, and stresses the importance of recording whatever dreams follow, regardless of whether they appear at first to be related to the request.

Patricia Garfield, *Creative Dreaming*, Ballantine Books, 1974, "inducing dreams" pp. 24-36. Garfield describes the frame of mind and physical conditions ideal for selecting a dream topic and successfully dreaming of what you have chosen.

Chapter 8   What to Expect From Here

Al Siebert, *The Survivor Personality*, Berkley/Perigee Books, 1996, pp. 29,36,170. Siebert describes the value to the individual's growth and evolution of electing to incorporate and value opposite or paradoxical characteristics within the self.

Lewis Engel and Tom Ferguson, *Imaginary Crimes: Why We Punish Ourselves and How to Stop*, Houghton Mifflin Company 1990, Running Away From Happiness: Why we Avoid Intimacy, Pleasure, and Sexual Fulfillment, pp. 146-168. This is a marvelous explanation of the phenomenon of the denial of happiness; how it masquerades as reason in our conscious thought patterns, and how we may decide to release ourselves from this living prison by becoming aware of these patterns and consciously indending to embrace life on new terms.

Index

Suggested Reading

Living Your Dreams by Dr. Gayle Delaney. Published by Harper & Row of San Francisco. This is one of the best possible in-depth primers for the serious student of dreams. It details the "interview" method of examining symbols for what they mean to the dreamer, and is very effective for becoming better able to help others or to unravel your own dreams.

Dream Work by Jeremy Taylor. Published by Paulist Press. This is an excellent study of Taylor's approach to interpretation and conducting dream groups. He tackles questions of religion, psychic phenomena, and social responsibility in a way that makes wonderful sense.

Our Dreaming Mind by Robert L. Van De Castle Ph.D. Published by Ballentine Books. A look at the research and history of dreams that is academically sound without being mind-numbing. Excellent resource for students, teachers and folks who want a broader look at the field of dreams.

Recurring Dreams A Journey to Wholeness by Kathleen Sullivan. Published by Crossing Press. The story of one woman's journey of discovery through journaling and deciphering her dreams. A wonderful example of working with images over time, and making dreamwork a sacred practice in your life.

Dreamcatching by Alan Siegel, Ph.D. and Kelly Bulkeley, Ph.D. Published by Three Rivers Press. This is reassuring and very helpful guide to children's dreams, and includes suggestions on how to support children in expressing their dreams with a light, non-intrusive touch.

The Healing Power of Dreams by Patricia Garfield, Ph.D. Published by Fireside of Simon and Schuster. An important exploration of dreams that reveal illness or physical problems, as well as reflect the road to healing and recovery.

The Dream Messenger by Patricia Garfield, Ph.D. Published by Simon and Schuster. This book looks at the patterns and gifts within our dreams of the departed. An excellent support for the newly bereaved, as well as those of us who are curious about our dreams of communicating with loved ones who have passed on.

Gillian Holloway holds an M.A. and Ph.D. in psychology and is dedicated to helping us all understand and benefit from our dreams.

At home in the Pacific Northwest, Dr. Holloway teaches courses in Dream Psychology and Intuition at Marylhurst University and leads private dream study groups. A popular media guest, Dr. Holloway has appeared on nationally syndicated radio programs such as Art Bell's *Dreamland* and television shows like ABC's *20/20*.

She writes a weekly advice column in *Woman's World Magazine* called "What Your Dreams Mean" which answers fascinating questions about what our dreams reveal. Her award winning website **Lifetreks.com** is one of the most respected Internet resources about the study of dreams. A member of the Association for the Study of Dreams and The National Speakers Association, she strives to increase awareness of the power of dreams to enrich and balance hectic lives.

If you have an unusual dream you'd like to share, or a story about how a dream has helped you, I would love to hear about it. You can contact me at the following address and through my website.

Gillian Holloway, Ph.D.
Lifetreks
PO Box 2487
Vancouver WA 98668
Email: gholloway@lifetreks.com

http://www.lifetreks.com

Special Dream Topics Available on Cassette
by
Gillian Holloway, Ph.D.

Remembering Dreams Better: The Gold in Your Subconscious
Methods for remembering dreams more easily and fully.

Why That Nightmare?
Explains the often surprising factors that contribute to nightmares and how to discover the often important and urgent information they contain.

Nights of Passion: Understanding Sexual Dreams
Almost all of us have sexual dreams, but few of us know much about what they mean or how we can benefit from them. This program answers questions you have always wondered about, and provides reassuring insights about our wildest dreams.

Dream Incubation: Asking for the Dreams You Want
This program reveals advanced techniques for eliciting dreams on special problems, important questions or decisions in your life.

That Dream Again: The Meaning of Recurring Dreams
Learn why recurring dreams are important to understand, and why you may be having a single dream for so many years.

Psychic Dreams
This program is a no-nonsense look at psychic elements in dreams that does not conflict with any theology or faith. You'll see how to benefit from extraordinary dreams and take a practical approach to the messages they contain.

Each tape runs one hour and costs $9.95 which includes postage. To order please send check or money order to:

Lifetreks
PO Box 2487
Vancouver WA 98668

Also Available from Practical Psychology Press:

The Survivor Personality

by Al Siebert, Ph.D.

How to cope with constant change, survive emergencies, gain strength from adversity, thrive under pressure, handle difficult people, recover from illness, and develop a talent for serendipity. Shows how the human race is in a transformation to its next level of development. Bernie Siegel, M.D., says, *"Read it! I loved it!"*

> Read excerpts at: *www.thrivenet.com*
> Soft cover, 1996, 294 pages, $12, ISBN 0-399-52230-1
> Credit Card orders call: 800/788-6262

The Adult Student's Guide to Survival & Success, 4th Edition

by Al Siebert, Ph.D., Bernadine Gilpin, M.A., and
*   Mary B. Karr, M.S.*

How to confront and overcome fears, gain family support, get financial help, balance work and college, study effectively, do well on tests, and increase self-confidence. A thrilled student says, *"This book is phenomenal! I'm getting A's in my courses and still have time for my job and my family!"*

> For more information, visit our Adult Student web site:
> *www.adultstudent.com*
>
> Soft cover, 2000, 176 pages, $15, ISBN 0-944227-20-1

Copies of *The Adult Student's Guide* or *Dreaming Insights* can be purchased from:

> *Independent Publisher's Group*
> *814 N. Franklin Street*
> *Chicago, IL 60610*
>
> *Phone: 800/888-4741*